THE FRAGMENTS OF
EMPEDOCLES

TRANSLATED INTO ENGLISH VERSE

BY

WILLIAM ELLERY LEONARD, Ph. D.

ENGLISH DEPARTMENT, UNIVERSITY OF WISCONSIN

CHICAGO

THE OPEN COURT PUBLISHING COMPANY

LONDON AGENTS

KEGAN PAUL, TRENCH, TRÜBNER & CO., LTD.

ISBN: 978-0-359-08989-5

Empedocles...
Whom that three-cornered isle of all the lands
Bore on her coasts....which, though for much she seem
The mighty and the wondrous isle,... hath ne'er
Possessed within her aught of more renown,
Nor aught more holy, wonderful, and dear
Than this true man. Nay, ever so far and pure
The lofty music of his breast divine
Lifts up its voice and tells of glories found
That scarce he seems of human stock create.

Lucretius, I. 716 ff.

DEDICATION.

(To W. R. N.)

In my last winter by Atlantic seas,
How often, when the long day's task was through,
I found, in nights of friendliness with you,
The quiet corner of the scholar's ease;
While you explored the Orphic liturgies,
Or old Pythagoras' mystic One and Two,
Or heartened me with Plato's larger view,
Or the world-epic of Empedocles:

It cost you little; but such things as these,
When man goes inland, following his star—
When man goes inland where the strangers are—
Build him a house of goodly memories:
So take this book in token, and rejoice
That I am richer having heard your voice.

W. E. L.
Madison. Wis., Dec. 1906.

PREFACE.

THIS translation was made at the suggestion of my friend, Dr. W. R. Newbold, Professor of Greek Philosophy at the University of Pennsylvania, in the hope of interesting here and there a student of thought or a lover of poetry. The introduction and notes are intended merely to illustrate the text: they touch only incidentally on the doxographical material and give thus by no means a complete account of all it is possible to know about Empedocles's philosophy. My indebtedness to the critics is frequently attested in the references; but I have in all points tried to exercise an independent judgment. Most citations from works not accessible in English are given in translation.

It is a genuine pleasure to acknowledge my special obligations to Professor Newbold and to Professor E. B. McGilvary of the philosophical department at Wisconsin for their kindness in reading the manuscript and adding several valuable suggestions. I am indebted to Dr. J. R. Blackman of the department of physiology at the University of Wisconsin for medical references.

WILLIAM ELLERY LEONARD.

MADISON, WIS., May 14, 1907.

TABLE OF CONTENTS.

THE FRAGMENTS OF EMPEDOCLES.

EMPEDOCLES: THE MAN, THE PHILOS-OPHER, THE POET.

LIFE.

THE philosopher Empedocles, according to the common tradition of antiquity, was born at Agrigentum in Sicily, and flourished just before the Peloponnesian war, the contemporary of the great Athenians about Pericles. He might have heard the *Prometheus* in the theatre of Dionysus and have talked with Euripides in the Agora; or have seen with Phidias the bright Pallas Athene on the Acropolis; or have listened in the groves beyond the city while Anaxagoras unfolded to him those half-spiritual guesses at the nature of the universe, so different from his own. He might: but the details of his life are all too imperfectly recorded. The brief references in other philosophers and the *vita* of Diogenes Laertius contain much that is contradictory or legendary. Though apparently of a wealthy and conservative family, he took the lead among his fellow citizens against the encroachments of the aristocracy; but, as it seems, falling at last from popular favor, he left Agrigentum and died in the Peloponnesus—his famous leap into Mount Aetna being as mythical as his reputed translation after a sacrificial meal.... But time restores the exiles: Florence at last set the image of Dante before the gates of Santa Croce;.and now, after two thousand years, the hardy democrats of Agrigentum begin to cherish (so I have read) the honest memory of Empedocles with that of Mazzini and Garibaldi.

PERSONALITY.

The personality of this old Mediterranean Greek must have been impressive. He was not only the statesman and philosopher, but the poet. And egotistic, melancholy, eloquent[1] soul that he was, he seems to have considered himself above all as the wonder-worker and the hierophant, in purple vest and golden girdle,

"Crowned both with fillets and with flowering wreaths;"

and he tells us of his triumphal passage through the Sicilian cities, how throngs of his men and women accompanied him along the road, how from house and alley thousands of the fearful and the sick crowded upon him and besought oracles or healing words. And stories have come down to us of his wonderful deeds, as the waking of a woman from a long trance and the quite plausible cure of a madman by music. Some traces of this imposing figure, with elements frankly drawn from legends not here mentioned appear in Arnold's poem.

[1] From Empedocles, indeed, according to Aristotle, the study of rhetoric got its first impulse. Cf. Diels's *Gorgias und Empedocles* in *Sitzungsberichte d. K. P. Akademie d. Wissenschaften*, 1884.

WORKS. *

Of the many works, imputed to Empedocles by antiquity, presumably only two are genuine, the poems *On Nature* and the *Purifications;* and of these we possess but the fragments preserved in the citations of philosopher and doxographer from Aristotle to Simplicius, which, though but a small part of the whole, are much more numerous and comprehensive than those of either Xenophanes or Parmenides. It is impossible to determine when the poems were lost: they were read doubtless by Lucretius and Cicero, possibly as late as the sixth century by Simplicius, who at least quotes from the *On Nature* at length.[2]

HISTORY OF THE TEXT.

The fragments were imperfectly collected late in the Renaissance, as far as I have been able to determine, first by the great German Xylander, who translated them into Latin. Stephanus published his *Empedoclis Fragmenta* at Paris in 1573. But not till the nineteenth century did they get the attention they deserve, in the editions of Sturz (1805) Karsten (1838), Stein (1852), and Mullach (1860), which show, however, confusing diversities in the readings as well as in the general arrangement. Each except Stein's is accompanied by Latin trans-

[2]The writings of Democritus are conjectured to have been lost between the third and fifth centuries.

lation[3] and notes. But our best text is unquestionably that of Hermann Diels of Berlin, first published in 1901 in his *Poetarum Philosophorum Fragmenta,* and subsequently (1906), with a few slight changes and additions, in his *Fragmente der Vorsokratiker.*

TRANSLATIONS.

As said above, there are several translations into Latin; all that I have seen being in prose, and some rather loose for the work of distinguished scholars. The late P. Tannery gives a literal French translation in his work on Hellenic Science, Diels in his *Fragmente* one in German, Bodrero in his *Il Principio* one in Italian, and Burnet and Fairbanks in their works on early Greek philosophy literal English translations, of which the former's is the better. There is one in German hexameters from the earlier decades of the last century; and a few brief selections in the English hexameters of W. C. Lawton may be found in Warner's *Library of the World's Best Literature.* The works of Frere and of Symonds contain specimen renderings, the former's in verse, the latter's in prose. Probably Diels does most justice to the meaning of Empedocles; none assuredly does any kind of justice to his poetry.

THE IDEAS OF EMPEDOCLES.

We can reconstruct something of Empedocles's system out of the fragments themselves and out of

---

[3] I have not seen the original of Sturz's edition; but I gather from references in my reading that it contains a translation.

the allusions in the ancients; yet our knowledge is by no means precise, and even from the earliest times has there been diversity of interpretation. Various problems are discussed, as they come up, in the Notes, but a brief survey of what seems to be his thought as a whole, even at the risk of some repetition, may help the general reader to get his bearings.

The philosophy of the *On Nature* may be considered as a union of the Eleatic doctrine of Being with that of the Heraclitic Becoming, albeit the Sicilian is more the natural scientist than the dialectician, more the Spencer than the Hegel of his times. With Parmenides he denies that the aught can come from or return to the naught; with Heraclitus he affirms the principle of development. There is no real creation or annihilation in this universal round of things; but an eternal mixing and unmixing, due to two eternal powers, Love and Hate, of one world-stuff in its sum unalterable and eternal. There is something in the conception suggestive of the chemistry of later times. To the water of Thales, the air of Anaximenes, and the fire of Heraclitus he adds earth, and declares them as all alike primeval, the promise and the potency of the universe,

"The fourfold root of all things."

These are the celebrated "four elements" of later philosophy and magic. In the beginning, if we may so speak of a vision which seems to transcend

time, these four, held together by the uniting bond
of Love, rested, each separated and unmixed, beside
one another in the shape of a perfect sphere, which
by the entrance of Hate was gradually broken up
to develop at last into the world and the individual
things,

"Knit in all forms and wonderful to see."

But the complete mastery of Hate, means the complete dissipation and destruction of things as such,
until Love, winning the upper hand, begins to unite
and form another world of life and beauty, which
ends in the still and lifeless sphere of old, again

"exultant in surrounding solitude."

Whereupon, in the same way, new world-periods
arise, and in continual interchange follow one another forever, like the secular æons of the nebular
hypothesis of to-day.

Moreover, Empedocles tells us of a mysterious
vortex, the origin of which he may have explained
in some lost portion of his poem, a whirling mass,
like the nebula in Orion or the original of our solar
system, that seems to be the first stage in the world-
process after the motionless harmony of the sphere.
Out of this came the elements one by one: first, air,
which, condensing or thickening, encompassed the
rest in the form of a globe or, as some maintain, of
an egg; then fire, which took the upper space, and
crowded air beneath her. And thus arose two
hemispheres, together forming the hollow vault of
the terrestrial heaven above and below us, the

bright entirely of fire, the dark of air, sprinkled with the patches of fire we call stars. And, because in unstable equilibrium, or because bearing still something of the swift motion of the vortex, or because of fire's intrinsic push and pressure—for Empedocles's physics are here particularly obscure—this vault begins to revolve: and behold the morning and the evening of the first day; for this revolution of the vault is, he tells us, the cause of day and night.

Out of the other elements came the earth, probably something warm and slimy, without form and void. It too was involved in the whirl of things; and the same force which expels the water from a sponge, when swung round and round in a boy's hand, worked within her, and the moist spurted forth and its evaporation filled the under spaces of air, and the dry land appeared. And the everlasting Law made two great lights, for signs and seasons, and for days and years, the greater light to rule the day, and the lesser light to rule the night; and it made the stars also.

The development of organic life, in which the interest of Empedocles chiefly centers, took place, as we have seen, in the period of the conflict of Love and Hate, through the unceasing mixing and separation of the four elements. Furthermore, the quantitative differences of the combinations produced qualitative differences of sensible properties. First the plants, conceived as endowed with feeling, sprang up, germinations out of earth. Then ani-

mals arose piecemeal—he tells us in one passage—
heads, arms, eyes, roaming ghastly through space,
the chance unions of which resulted in grotesque
shapes until joined in fit number and proportion,
they developed into the organisms we see about us.
In another passage we hear how first rose mere
lumps of earth

"with rude impress,"

but he is probably speaking of two separate periods
of creation.   Empedocles was a crude evolutionist.[4]
His theory of the attraction of like for like, so
suggestive of the chemical affinities of modern science; his theory of perception, the earliest recog-
nition, with the possible exception of Alcmäon of
Croton, of the subjective element in man's experience with the outer world; and his affirmation of
the consciousness of matter, in company with so
many later materialists, even down to Haeckel, who
puts the soul in the atom, are, perhaps, for our purposes sufficiently explained in the notes.
Behind all the absurdities of the system of Empedocles, we recognize the keen observation, in-
sight, and generalizing power of a profound mind,
which, in our day with our resources of knowledge,
would have been in the forefront of the world's seek-
ers after that Reality which even the last and the
greatest seek with a success too humble to warrant
much smiling at those gone before.

[4] Some portions of the above paragraphs are translated and con-
densed from Zeller, some others from Vorländer, *Geschichte der
Philosophie*, I. Band, Leipsic, 1903.

THE POETRY OF EMPEDOCLES.

Empedocles and his forerunner Parmenides were the only Greek philosophers who wrote down their systems in verse; for Heraclitus had written in crabbed prose, and Xenophanes was more poet-satirist than poet-philosopher. Lucretius, the poetical disciple of Empedocles (though not in the same degree that he was the philosophic disciple of Epicurus), is in this their only successor. Contemporary reflective satire and the metrical forms of the Orphics may, as Burnet conjectures, have suggested the innovation; but both Parmenides and Empedocles were poets by nature, and I see no reason why they should not naturally and spontaneously have chosen the poet's splendid privilege of verse for their thought.

The Ionic dialect of Empedocles's hexameters, and occasionally even his phrase, is Homeric; but in mood and manner, as sometimes in philosophic terminology, he recalls the Eleatic. Parmenides had written:

> "And thou shalt know the Source etherial,
> And all the starry signs along the sky,
> And the resplendent works of that clear lamp
> Of glowing sun, and whence they all arose.
> Likewise of wandering works of round-eyed moon
> Shalt thou yet learn and of her source; and then
> Shalt thou know too the heavens that close us round—
> Both whence they sprang and how Fate leading them
> Bound fast to keep the limits of the stars....
> How earth and sun and moon and common sky,
> The Milky Way, Olympos outermost,
> And burning might of stars made haste to be."[8]

[8] Parmenides, fr. 10, 11, Diels, FV.

And it is as if he were addressing the Agrigen-
tine and bequeathing him his spiritual heritage;
and we might add thereto those verses of another
poet of more familiar times:

> "And thou shalt write a song like mine, and yet
> Much more than mine, as thou art more than I."

For, although Empedocles has left us no passage of the gorgeous imagination of Parmenides's
proem,[6] the ἵπποι ταί με φέρουσιν, his fragments as
a whole seem much more worth while.

He was true poet. There is first the grandeur
of his conception. Its untruth for the intellect of
to-day should not blind us to its truth and power
for the imagination, the same yesterday, to-day and
perhaps forever. The Ptolemaic astronomy of *Par-
adise Lost* is as real to the student of Milton as the
Copernican to the student of Laplace, and an essen-
tial element in the poem. The nine circles of the
subterranean Abyss lose none of their impressive-
ness for us because we know more of geology than
the author of the *Inferno*. The imagination can
glory in the cross of Christ, towering over the
wrecks of time, long after the intellect has settled
with the dogmas of orthodoxy. And an idea may
be imposing even for the intellect where the intellect repudiates its validity. A stupendous error
like the Hegelian logic of history, even the pseudo-
science of Goethe's vertebral theory of the skull,
that yet suggests the great principle of morpholog-

---

[6] Diels, *FV*. Arnold has borrowed from it one of the best lines
of *Empedocles on Aetna*:
"Ye sun-born Virgins! on the road of truth."—

ical and functional metamorphosis, argues greater things for the mind of man than any truth, however ingeniously discovered, in the world of petty facts. And the response of the soul is a poetic response, the thrill and the enthusiasm before the large idea. Our poet's conception is impressive to imagination and to intellect: we stand with him amid the awful silence of the primeval Sphere that yet exults in surrounding solitude; but out of the darkness and the abyss there comes a sound: one by one do quake the limbs of God; the powers of life and death are at work; Love and Hate contend in the bosom of nature as in the bosom of man; we sweep on in fire and rain and down the

"awful heights of Air;"

amid the monstrous shapes, the arms, the heads, the glaring eyes, in space, and at last we are in the habitable world, this shaggy earth, this sky-roofed cave of the fruitful vine and olive, of the multitudinous tribes of hairy beasts, and of men and women,—all wonderful to see; for Empedocles is strikingly concrete. But the æons of change never end; and the revolution, as we have seen, comes full circle forever.

There is too the large poet's feeling for the color, the movement, the mystery, the life of the world about us: for the wide glow of blue heaven, for the rain streaming down on the mountain trees, for the wind-storm riding in from ocean, for

"Night, the lonely, with her sightless eyes,"

for the lion couched on the mountain side, the diver-
bird skimming the waves with its wings, and

"The songless shoals of spawning fish"

that are

"nourished in deep waters"

and led, it may be, by Aphrodite.

There is the poet's relation to his kind, the sym-
pathy with

"men and women, the pitied and bewailed,"

who after their little share of life with briefest
fates

"Like smoke are lifted up and flit away;"

the interest and the joy in the activities of man:
how now one lights his lantern and sallies forth in
the wintry night; how now another mixes his paints
in the sunlight for a variegated picture of trees
and birds which is to adorn the temple; how now
a little girl, down by the brook,

"Plays with a waterclock of gleaming bronze."

There is the poet's instinct for the effective
phrase, which suggests so much, because it tells so
little; an austere simplicity, which relates the author
by achievement to that best period of Greek art to
which he belonged by birth; and a roll of rhythm
as impassioned and sonorous as was ever heard on
Italian soil, though that soil was the birth-place of
Lucretius...But I am the translator, not the critic,
of the poet.

BIBLIOGRAPHY.

BODRERO in his *Il Principio fondamentale del sistema di Empedocle*[1] (Rome, 1904; cited as "Bodrero") gives a valuable bibliography, almost exhaustive for the study of our philosopher, save for the surprising omission of the work of Burnet. Bodrero is presumably known and accessible to the special student; for the general reader the following will, perhaps, be found sufficient:

BLAKEWELL. *Source Book in Greek Philosophy*, New York, 1907. (Contains partial prose translation, but came to hand after the present volume was in press.)

BURNET, *Early Greek Philosophy*, London, 1892. (Keen and independent. Cited as "Burnet.").

FAIRBANKS, *The First Philosophers of Greece*, New York, 1898. (Contains translations of the doxographers on Empedocles.)

GOMPERZ, *Greek Thinkers*, vol. I., trans. by Laurie Magnus, New York, 1901. (Beautifully written, inspiring; but somewhat fanciful. Cited as "Gomperz.")

SYMONDS, *Studies of the Greek Poets*, vol. I., chap. VII., London, 1893. (Good critical appreciation, with some prose translations.)

TANNERY, *Pour l'histoire de la science hellène*, Paris, 1887. (Keen and independent. Cited as "Tannery.")

WINDELBAND, *History of Ancient Philosophy*, trans. by H. E. Cushman, New York, 1899.

---

[1] This book seems to me as remarkable for its scholarship and acumen as for the speciousness of its views. I wrote to Professor Diels about it, who answered, however, that he had not as yet found time to examine it.

ZELLER, *Die Philosophie der Griechen*, I. Teil, fünfte Auflage, Leipsic, 1892. (Cited as "Zeller.")

And the above mentioned texts of

DIELS, *Poetarum Philosophorum Fragmenta*, Berlin, 1901. (Contains the comments of the doxographers in the Greek, and a few, but very useful, original notes in Latin. Cited as "Diels, PPF.")

"   *Fragmente der Vorsokratiker*, zweite Auflage, erster Band, Berlin, 1906. (Contains German translation. Cited as "Diels, FV.")

ON NATURE.

To His Friend.

I.

Παυσανίη, σὺ δὲ κλῦθι, δαΐφρονος Ἀγχίτου υἱέ.

Hear thou, Pausanias, son of wise Anchitus!

Limitations of Knowledge.

2.

στεινωποὶ μὲν γὰρ παλάμαι κατὰ γυῖα κέχυνται·
πολλὰ δὲ δείλ᾽ ἔμπαια, τά τ᾽ ἀμβλύνουσι μερίμνας.
παῦρον δὲ ζωῆς ἰδίου μέρος ἀθρήσαντες
ὠκύμοροι καπνοῖο δίκην ἀρθέντες ἀπέπταν
αὐτὸ μόνον πεισθέντες, ὅτωι προσέκυρσεν ἕκαστος
πάντοσ᾽ ἐλαυνόμενοι, τὸ δ᾽ ὅλον [πᾶς] εὔχεται εὑρεῖν·
οὕτως οὔτ᾽ ἐπιδερκτὰ τάδ᾽ ἀνδράσιν οὐδ᾽ ἐπακουστά
οὔτε νόωι περιληπτά. σὺ δ᾽ οὖν, ἐπεὶ ὧδ᾽ ἐλιάσθης,
πεύσεαι οὐ πλέον ἠὲ βροτείη μῆτις ὄρωρεν.

For narrow through their members scattered ways
Of knowing lie. And many a vile surprise
Blunts soul and keen desire. And having viewed
Their little share of life, with briefest fates,
Like smoke they are lifted up and flit away,
Believing only what each chances on,

Hither and thither driven; yet they boast
The larger vision of the whole and all.
But thuswise never shall these things be seen,
Never be heard by men, nor seized by mind;
And thou, since hither now withdrawn apart,
Shalt learn—no more than mortal ken may span.

3.

στεγάσαι φρενὸς ἔλλοπος εἴσω.

Shelter these teachings in thine own mute breast.

4.

ἀλλὰ θεοὶ τῶν μὲν μανίην ἀποτρέψατε γλώσσης,
ἐκ δ᾽ ὁσίων στομάτων καθαρὴν ὀχετεύσατε πηγήν.
καὶ σέ, πολυμνήστη λευκώλενε παρθένε Μοῦσα,
ἄντομαι, ὧν θέμις ἐστὶν ἐφημερίοισιν ἀκούειν,
πέμπε παρ᾽ Εὐσεβίης ἐλάουσ᾽ εὐήνιον ἅρμα.
μηδέ σέ γ᾽ εὐδόξοιο βιήσεται ἄνθεα τιμῆς
πρὸς θνητῶν ἀνελέσθαι, ἐφ᾽ ὧι θ᾽ ὁσίης πλέον εἰπεῖν
θάρσεϊ καὶ τότε δὴ σοφίης ἐπ᾽ ἄκροισι θοάζειν.
ἀλλ᾽ ἄγ᾽ ἄθρει πάσηι παλάμηι, πῆι δῆλον ἕκαστον,
μήτε τι ὄψιν ἔχων πίστει πλέον ἢ κατ᾽ ἀκουήν
ἢ ἀκοὴν ἐρίδουπον ὑπὲρ τρανώματα γλώσσης,
μήτε τι τῶν ἄλλων, ὁπόσηι πόρος ἐστὶ νοῆσαι,
γυίων πίστιν ἔρυκε, νόει θ᾽ ἧι δῆλον ἕκαστον.

But turn their madness, Gods! from tongue of mine,
And drain through holy lips the well-spring clear!
And many-wooed, O white-armed Maiden-Muse,
Thee I approach: O drive and send to me
Meek Piety's well-reined chariot of song,

So far as lawful is for men to hear,
Whose lives are but a day.   Nor shall desire
To pluck the flowers of fame and wide report
Among mankind impel thee on to dare
Speech beyond holy bound and seat profane
Upon those topmost pinnacles of Truth.
But come, by every way of knowing see
How each thing is revealed.   Nor, having sight,
Trust sight no more than hearing will bear out,
Trust echoing ear but after tasting tongue;
Nor check the proof of all thy members aught:
Note by all ways each thing as 'tis revealed.

5.

ἀλλὰ κακοῖς μὲν κάρτα μέλει κρατέουσιν ἀπιστεῖν.
ὡς δὲ παρ' ἡμετέρης κέλεται πιστώματα Μούσης,
γνῶθι διασσηθέντος ἐνὶ σπλάγχνοισι λόγοιο.

Yea, but the base distrust the High and Strong;
Yet know the pledges that our Muse will urge,
When once her words be sifted through thy soul.

The Elements.

6.

τέσσαρα γὰρ πάντων ῥιζώματα πρῶτον ἄκουε·
Ζεὺς ἀργὴς Ἥρη τε φερέσβιος ἠδ' Ἀιδωνεύς
Νῆστίς θ', ἣ δακρύοις τέγγει κρούνωμα βρότειον.

And first the fourfold root of all things hear!—
White gleaming Zeus, life-bringing Here, Dis,
And Nestis whose tears bedew mortality.

7.

ἀγένητα.

The uncreated elements.

Birth and Death.

8.

ἄλλο δέ τοι ἐρέω· φύσις οὐδενός ἐστιν ἁπάντων
θνητῶν, οὐδέ τις οὐλομένου θανάτοιο τελευτή,
ἀλλὰ μόνον μίξις τε διάλλαξίς τε μιγέντων
ἐστί, φύσις δ' ἐπὶ τοῖς ὀνομάζεται ἀνθρώποισιν.

More will I tell thee too: there is no birth
Of all things mortal, nor end in ruinous death;
But mingling only and interchange of mixed
There is, and birth is but its name with men.

9.

οἱ δ' ὅτε μὲν κατὰ φῶτα μιγέντ' εἰς αἰθέρ' ἵ[κωνται]
ἢ κατὰ θηρῶν ἀγροτέρων γένος ἢ κατὰ θάμνων
ἠὲ κατ' οἰωνῶν, τότε μὲν τὸ [λέγουσι] γενέσθαι·
εὖτε δ' ἀποκρινθῶσι, τὰ δ' αὖ δυσδαίμονα πότμον·
ἢ θέμις [οὐ] καλέουσι, νόμωι δ' ἐπίφημι καὶ αὐτός.

But when in man, wild beast, or bird, or bush,
These elements commingle and arrive
The realms of light, the thoughtless deem it "birth";
When they dispart, 'tis "doom of death;" and though
Not this the Law, I too assent to use.

10.

θάνατον . . . ἀλοίτην.

Avenging Death.

Ex nihilo nihil.

II.

νήπιοι· οὐ γάρ σφιν δολιχόφρονές εἰσι μέριμναι,
οἳ δὴ γίγνεσθαι πάρος οὐκ ἐὸν ἐλπίζουσιν
ἤ τι καταθνήισκειν τε καὶ ἐξόλλυσθαι ἀπάντηι.

Fools! for their thoughts are briefly brooded o'er.
Who trust that what is not can e'er become,
Or aught that is can wholly die away.

12.

ἔκ τε γὰρ οὐδάμ' ἐόντος ἀμήχανόν ἐστι γενέσθαι
καί τ' ἐὸν ἐξαπολέσθαι ἀνήνυστον καὶ ἄπυστον·
αἰεὶ γὰρ τῆι γ' ἔσται, ὅπηι κέ τις αἰὲν ἐρείδηι.

From what-is-not what-is can ne'er become;
So that what-is should e'er be all destroyed,
No force could compass and no ear hath heard—
For there 'twill be forever where 'tis set.

The Plenum.

13.

οὐδέ τι τοῦ παντὸς κενεὸν πέλει οὐδὲ περισσόν.

The All hath neither Void nor Overflow.

14.

τοῦ παντὸς δ' οὐδὲν κενεόν· πόθεν οὖν τί κ' ἐπέλθοι;

But with the All there is no Void, so whence
Could aught of more come nigh?

Our Elements Immortal.

15.

οὐκ ἂν ἀνὴρ τοιαῦτα σοφὸς φρεσὶ μαντεύσαιτο,
ὡς ὄφρα μέν τε βιῶσι, τὸ δὴ βίοτον καλέουσι,
τόφρα μὲν οὖν εἰσίν, καί σφιν πάρα δειλὰ καὶ ἐσθλά,
πρὶν δὲ πάγεν τε βροτοὶ καὶ [ἐπεὶ] λύθεν, οὐδὲν ἄρ᾽ εἰσιν.

No wise man dreams such folly in his heart,
That only whilst we live what men call life
We have our being and take our good and ill,
And ere as mortals we compacted be,
And when as mortals we be loosed apart,
We are as nothing.

Love and Hate, the Everlasting.

16.

ἦι γὰρ καὶ πάρος ἔσκε, καὶ ἔσσεται, οὐδέ ποτ᾽, οἴω,
τούτων ἀμφοτέρων κενεώσεται ἄσπετος αἰών.

For even as Love and Hate were strong of yore,
They shall have their hereafter; nor I think
Shall endless Age be emptied of these Twain.

The Cosmic Process.

17.

δίπλ᾽ ἐρέω· τοτὲ μὲν γὰρ ἓν ηὐξήθη μόνον εἶναι
ἐκ πλεόνων, τοτὲ δ᾽ αὖ διέφυ πλέον᾽ ἐξ ἑνὸς εἶναι.
δοιὴ δὲ θνητῶν γένεσις, δοιὴ δ᾽ ἀπόλειψις·
τὴν μὲν γὰρ πάντων σύνοδος τίκτει τ᾽ ὀλέκει τε,
ἡ δὲ πάλιν διαφυομένων θρεφθεῖσα διέπτη.
καὶ ταῦτ᾽ ἀλλάσσοντα διαμπερὲς οὐδαμὰ λήγει,
ἄλλοτε μὲν Φιλότητι συνερχόμεν᾽ εἰς ἓν ἅπαντα,

ἄλλοτε δ' αὖ δίχ' ἕκαστα φορεύμενα Νείκεος ἔχθει.
[οὕτως ἧι μὲν ἓν ἐκ πλεόνων μεμάθηκε φύεσθαι]
ἠδὲ πάλιν διαφύντος ἑνὸς πλέον' ἐκτελέθουσι,
τῆι μὲν γίγνονταί τε καὶ οὔ σφισιν ἔμπεδος αἰών·
ἧι δὲ διαλλάσσοντα διαμπερὲς οὐδαμὰ λήγει,
ταύτηι δ' αἰὲν ἔασιν ἀκίνητοι κατὰ κύκλον.
ἀλλ' ἄγε μύθων κλῦθι· μάθη γάρ τοι φρένας αὔξει·
ὡς γὰρ καὶ πρὶν ἔειπα πιφαύσκων πείρατα μύθων,
δίπλ' ἐρέω· τοτὲ μὲν γὰρ ἓν ηὐξήθη μόνον εἶναι
ἐκ πλεόνων, τοτὲ δ' αὖ διέφυ πλέον' ἐξ ἑνὸς εἶναι,
πῦρ καὶ ὕδωρ καὶ γαῖα καὶ ἠέρος ἄπλετον ὕψος,
Νεῖκός τ' οὐλόμενον δίχα τῶν, ἀτάλαντον ἀπάντηι,
καὶ Φιλότης ἐν τοῖσιν, ἴση μῆκός τε πλάτος τε·
τὴν σὺ νόωι δέρκευ, μηδ' ὄμμασιν ἧσο τεθηπώς·
ἥτις καὶ θνητοῖσι νομίζεται ἔμφυτος ἄρθροις,
τῆι τε φίλα φρονέουσι καὶ ἄρθμια ἔργα τελοῦσι,
Γηθοσύνην καλέοντες ἐπώνυμον ἠδ' Ἀφροδίτην·
τὴν οὔ τις μετὰ τοῖσιν ἑλισσομένην δεδάηκε
θνητὸς ἀνήρ· σὺ δ' ἄκουε λόγου στόλον οὐκ ἀπατηλόν.
ταῦτα γὰρ ἰσά τε πάντα καὶ ἥλικα γένναν ἔασι,
τιμῆς δ' ἄλλης ἄλλο μέδει, πάρα δ' ἦθος ἑκάστωι,
ἐν δὲ μέρει κρατέουσι περιπλομένοιο χρόνοιο.
καὶ πρὸς τοῖς οὔτ' ἄρ τέ τι γίνεται οὔτ' ἀπολήγει·
εἴτε γὰρ ἐφθείροντο διαμπερές, οὐκέτ' ἂν ἦσαν·
τοῦτο δ' ἐπαυξήσειε τὸ πᾶν τί κε καὶ πόθεν ἐλθόν;
πῆι δέ κε κἠξαπόλοιτο, ἐπεὶ τῶνδ' οὐδὲν ἔρημον;
ἀλλ' αὐτὰ ἔστιν ταῦτα, δι' ἀλλήλων δὲ θέοντα
γίγνεται ἄλλοτε ἄλλα καὶ ἠνεκὲς αἰὲν ὁμοῖα.

I will report a twofold truth. Now grows
The One from Many into being, now

Even from the One disparting come the Many.
Twofold the birth, twofold the death of things:
For, now, the meeting of the Many brings
To birth and death; and, now, whatever grew
From out their sundering, flies apart and dies.
And this long interchange shall never end.
Whiles into One do all through Love unite;
Whiles too the same are rent through hate of Strife.
And in so far as is the One still wont
To grow from Many, and the Many, again,
Spring from primeval scattering of the One,
So far have they a birth and mortal date;
And in so far as the long interchange
Ends not, so far forever established gods
Around the circle of the world they move.
But come! but hear my words! For knowledge
    gained
Makes strong thy soul. For as before I spake,
Naming the utter goal of these my words,
I will report a twofold truth. Now grows
The One from Many into being, now
Even from the One disparting come the Many,—
Fire, Water, Earth and awful heights of Air;
And shut from them apart, the deadly Strife
In equipoise, and Love within their midst
In all her being in length and breadth the same.
Behold her now with mind, and sit not there
With eyes astonished, for 'tis she inborn
Abides established in the limbs of men.
Through her they cherish thoughts of love, through
    her

Perfect the works of concord, calling her
By name Delight or Aphrodite clear.
She speeds revolving in the elements,
But this no mortal man hath ever learned—
Hear thou the undelusive course of proof:
Behold those elements own equal strength
And equal origin; each rules its task;
And unto each its primal mode; and each
Prevailing conquers with revolving time.
And more than these there is no birth nor end;
For were they wasted ever and evermore,
They were no longer, and the great All were then
How to be plenished and from what far coast?
And how, besides, might they to ruin come,
Since nothing lives that empty is of them?—
No, these are all, and, as they course along
Through one another, now this, now that is born—
And so forever down Eternity.

18.

Φιλίη.

Love.

19.

σχεδύνην Φιλότητα.

Firm-clasping Lovingness.

Love and Hate in the Organic World.

20.

τοῦτο μὲν ἂν βροτέων μελέων ἀριδείκετον ὄγκον·
ἄλλοτε μὲν Φιλότητι συνερχόμεν' εἰς ἓν ἅπαντα

γυῖα, τὰ σῶμα λέλογχε, βίου θαλέθοντος ἐν ἀκμῆι·
ἄλλοτε δ' αὖτε κακῆισι διατμηθέντ' 'Ερίδεσσι
πλάζεται ἄνδιχ' ἔκαστα περιρρηγμῖνι βίοιο.
ὡς δ' αὖτως θάμνοισι καὶ ἰχθύσιν ὑδρομελάθροις
θηρσί τ' ὀρειλεχέεσσιν ἰδὲ πτεροβάμοσι κύμβαις.

The world-wide warfare of the eternal Two
Well in the mass of human limbs is shown:
Whiles into one do they through Love unite,
And mortal members take the body's form,
And life doth flower at the prime; and whiles,
Again dissevered by the Hates perverse,
They wander far and wide and up and down
The surf-swept beaches and drear shores of life.
So too with thicket, tree, and gleaming fish
Housed in the crystal walls of waters wide;
And so with beasts that couch on mountain slopes,
And water-fowls that skim the long blue sea.

From the Elements is All We See.

21.

ἀλλ' ἄγε, τῶνδ' ὀάρων προτέρων ἐπιμάρτυρα δέρκευ,
εἴ τι καὶ ἐν προτέροισι λιπόξυλον ἔπλετο μορφῆι,
ἠέλιον μὲν θερμὸν ὁρᾶν καὶ λαμπρὸν ἀπάντηι,
ἄμβροτα δ' ὅσσ' ἴδει τε καὶ ἀργέτι δεύεται αὐγῆι,
ὄμβρον δ' ἐν πᾶσι δνοφόεντά τε ῥιγαλέον τε·
ἐκ δ' αἴης προρέουσι θέλυμνά τε καὶ στερεωπά.
ἐν δὲ Κότωι διάμορφα καὶ ἄνδιχα πάντα πέλονται,
σὺν δ' ἔβη ἐν Φιλότητι καὶ ἀλλήλοισι ποθεῖται.
ἐκ τούτων γὰρ πάνθ' ὅσα τ' ἦν ὅσα τ' ἔστι καὶ ἔσται,
δένδρεά τ' ἐβλάστησε καὶ ἀνέρες ἠδὲ γυναῖκες,

θῆρές τ᾽ οἰωνοί τε καὶ ὑδατοθρέμμονες ἰχθῦς,
καί τε θεοὶ δολιχαίωνες τιμῆισι φέριστοι.
αὐτὰ γὰρ ἔστιν ταῦτα, δι᾽ ἀλλήλων δὲ θέοντα
γίγνεται ἀλλοιωπά· τόσον διὰ κρῆσις ἀμείβει.

But come, and to my words foresaid look well,
If their wide witness anywhere forgot
Aught that behooves the elemental forms:
Behold the Sun, the warm, the bright-diffused;
Behold the eternal Stars, forever steeped
In liquid heat and glowing radiance; see
Also the Rain, obscure and cold and dark,
And how from Earth streams forth the Green and
    Firm.
And all through Wrath are split to shapes diverse;
And each through Love draws near and yearns for
    each.
For from these elements hath budded all
That was or is or evermore shall be—
All trees, and men and women, beasts and birds,
And fishes nourished in deep waters, aye,
The long-lived gods, in honors excellent.
For these are all, and, as they course along
Through one another, they take new faces all,
By varied mingling and enduring change.

Similia Similibus.

22.

ἄρθμια μὲν γὰρ ταῦτα ἑαυτῶν πάντα μέρεσσιν,
ἠλέκτωρ τε χθών τε καὶ οὐρανὸς ἠδὲ θάλασσα,
ὅσσα φιν ἐν θνητοῖσιν ἀποπλαχθέντα πέφυκεν.

ὡς δ' αὔτως ὅσα κρᾶσιν ἐπαρκέα μᾶλλον ἔασιν,
ἀλλήλοις ἔστερκται ὁμοιωθέντ' 'Αφροδίτηι.
ἐχθρὰ [δ' ἃ] πλεῖστον ἀπ' ἀλλήλων διέχουσι μάλιστα
γέννηι τε κρήσει τε καὶ εἴδεσιν ἐκμάκτοισι,
πάντηι συγγίνεσθαι ἀήθεα καὶ μάλα λυγρά
Νείκεος ἐννεσίηισιν, ὅτι σφίσι γένναν ἔοργεν.

For amber Sun and Earth and Heaven and Sea
Is friendly with its every part that springs,
Far driven and scattered, in the mortal world;
So too those things that are most apt to mix
Are like, and love by Aphrodite's hest.
But hostile chiefly are those things which most
From one another differ, both in birth,
And in their mixing and their molded forms—
Unwont to mingle, miserable and lone,
After the counsels of their father, Hate.

An Analogy.

23.

ὡς δ' ὁπόταν γραφέες ἀναθήματα ποικίλλωσιν
ἀνέρες ἀμφὶ τέχνης ὑπὸ μήτιος εὖ δεδαῶτε,
οἵτ' ἐπεὶ οὖν μάρψωσι πολύχροα φάρμακα χερσίν,
ἁρμονίηι μείξαντε τὰ μὲν πλέω, ἄλλα δ' ἐλάσσω,
ἐκ τῶν εἴδεα πᾶσιν ἀλίγκια πορσύνουσι,
δένδρεά τε κτίζοντε καὶ ἀνέρας ἠδὲ γυναῖκας
θῆράς τ' οἰωνούς τε καὶ ὑδατοθρέμμονας ἰχθῦς
καί τε θεοὺς δολιχαίωνας τιμῆισι φερίστους·
οὕτω μή σ' ἀπάτη φρένα καινύτω ἄλλοθεν εἶναι
θνητῶν, ὅσσα γε δῆλα γεγάκασιν ἄσπετα, πηγήν,
ἀλλὰ τορῶς ταῦτ' ἴσθι, θεοῦ πάρα μῦθον ἀκούσας.

And even as artists—men who know their craft
Through wits of cunning—paint with streak and
    hue
Bright temple-tablets, and will seize in hand
The oozy poisons pied and red and gold
(Mixing harmonious, now more, now less),
From which they fashion forms innumerable,
And like to all things, peopling a fresh world
With trees, and men and women, beasts and birds,
And fishes nourished in deep waters, aye,
And long-lived gods in honors excellent:
Just so (and let no guile deceive thy breast),
Even so the spring of mortal things, leastwise
Of all the host born visible to man.
O guard this knowledge well, for thou hast heard
In this my song the Goddess and her tale.

The Speculative Thinker.

24.

. . . κορυφὰς ἑτέρας ἑτέρηισι προσάπτων
μύθων μὴ τελέειν ἀτραπὸν μίαν. . .

To join together diverse peaks of thought,
And not complete one road that has no turn.

An Aphorism.

25.

. . . καὶ δὶς γάρ, ὃ δεῖ, καλόν ἐστιν ἐνισπεῖν.

What must be said, may well be said twice o'er.

The Law of the Elements.

26.

ἐν δὲ μέρει κρατέουσι περιπλομένοιο κύκλοιο,
καὶ φθίνει εἰς ἄλληλα καὶ αὔξεται ἐν μέρει αἴσης.
αὐτὰ γὰρ ἔστιν ταῦτα, δι' ἀλλήλων δὲ θέοντα
γίνονται ἄνθρωποί τε καὶ ἄλλων ἔθνεα θηρῶν
ἄλλοτε μὲν Φιλότητι συνερχόμεν' εἰς ἕνα κόσμον,
ἄλλοτε δ' αὖ δίχ' ἕκαστα φορούμενα Νείκεος ἔχθει,
εἰσόκεν ἓν συμφύντα τὸ πᾶν ὑπένερθε γένηται.
οὕτως ἦι μὲν ἓν ἐκ πλεόνων μεμάθηκε φύεσθαι,
ἠδὲ πάλιν διαφύντος ἑνὸς πλέον' ἐκτελέθουσι,
τῆι μὲν γίγνονταί τε καὶ οὔ σφισιν ἔμπεδος αἰών·
ἦι δὲ τάδ' ἀλλάσσοντα διαμπερὲς οὐδαμὰ λήγει,
ταύτηι δ' αἰὲν ἔασιν ἀκίνητοι κατὰ κύκλον.

In turn they conquer as the cycles roll,
And wane the one to other still, and wax
The one to other in turn by olden Fate;
For these are all, and, as they course along
Through one another, they become both men
And multitudinous tribes of hairy beasts;
Whiles in fair order through Love united all,
Whiles rent asunder by the hate of Strife,
Till they, when grown into the One and All
Once more, once more go under and succumb.
And in so far as is the One still wont
To grow from the Many, and the Many, again,
Spring from primeval scattering of the One,
So far have they a birth and mortal date.
And in so far as this long interchange
Ends not, so far forever established gods
Around the circle of the world they move.

The Sphere. ●

27.

ἔνθ' οὔτ' Ἠελίοιο διείδεται ὠκέα γυῖα
οὐδὲ μὲν οὐδ' αἴης λάσιον μένος οὐδὲ θάλασσα·
οὕτως Ἁρμονίης πυκινῶι κρύφωι ἐστήρικται
Σφαῖρος κυκλοτερὴς μονίηι περιηγέι γαίων.

There views one not the swift limbs of the Sun,
Nor there the strength of shaggy Earth, nor Sea;
But in the strong recess of Harmony,
Established firm abides the rounded Sphere,
Exultant in surrounding solitude.

27a.

οὐ στάσις οὐδέ τε δῆρις ἀναίσιμος ἐν μελέεσσιν.

Nor faction nor fight unseemly in its limbs.

28.

ἀλλ' ὅ γε πάντοθεν ἶσος [ἔην] καὶ πάμπαν ἀπείρων
Σφαῖρος κυκλοτερὴς μονίηι περιηγέι γαίων.

The Sphere on every side the boundless same,
Exultant in surrounding solitude.

29.

οὐ γὰρ ἀπὸ νώτοιο δύο κλάδοι ἀίσσονται,
οὐ πόδες, οὐ θοὰ γοῦνα, οὐ μήδεα γεννήεντα,
ἀλλὰ σφαῖρος ἔην καὶ [πάντοθεν] ἶσος ἑαυτῶι.

For from its back there swing no branching arms,
It hath no feet nor knees alert, nor form

Of life-producing member,—on all sides
A sphere it was, and like unto itself.

30.

αὐτὰρ ἐπεὶ μέγα Νεῖκος ἐνὶμμελέεσσιν ἐθρέφθη
ἐς τιμάς τ' ἀνόρουσε τελειομένοιο χρόνοιο,
ὅς σφιν ἀμοιβαῖος πλατέος παρ' ἐλήλαται ὅρκου...

Yet after mighty Strife had waxen great
Within the members of the Sphere, and rose
To her own honors, as the times arrived
Which unto each in turn, to Strife, to Love,
Should come by amplest oath and old decree...

31.

πάντα γὰρ ἐξείης πελεμίζετο γυῖα θεοῖο.

For one by one did quake the limbs of God.

Physical Analogies.

32.

δύω δέει ἄρθρον.

The joint binds two.

33.

ὡς δ' ὅτ' ὀπὸς γάλα λευκὸν ἐγόμφωσεν καὶ ἔδησε...

But as when rennet of the fig-tree juice
Curdles the white milk, and will bind it fast...

34.

ἄλφιτον ὕδατι κολλήσας...

Cementing meal with water...

The Conquest of Love.

35.

αὐτὰρ ἐγὼ παλίνορσος ἐλεύσομαι ἐς πόρον ὕμνων,
τὸν πρότερον κατέλεξα, λόγου λόγον ἐξοχετεύων,
κεῖνον· ἐπεὶ Νεῖκος μὲν ἐνέρτατον ἵκετο βένθος
δίνης, ἐν δὲ μέσηι Φιλότης στροφάλιγγι γένηται,
ἐν τῆι δὴ τάδε πάντα συνέρχεται ἓν μόνον εἶναι,
οὐκ ἄφαρ, ἀλλὰ θελημὰ συνιστάμεν' ἄλλοθεν ἄλλα.
τῶν δέ τε μισγομένων χεῖτ' ἔθνεα μυρία θνητῶν·
πολλὰ δ' ἄμεικτ' ἔστηκε κεραιομένοισιν ἐναλλάξ,
ὅσσ' ἔτι Νεῖκος ἔρυκε μετάρσιον· οὐ γὰρ ἀμεμφέως
τῶν πᾶν ἐξέστηκεν ἐπ' ἔσχατα τέρματα κύκλου,
ἀλλὰ τὰ μέν τ' ἐνέμιμνε, μελέων τὰ δέ τ' ἐξεβεβήκει.
ὅσσον δ' αἰὲν ὑπεκπροθέοι, τόσον αἰὲν ἐπήιει
ἠπιόφρων Φιλότητος ἀμεμφέος ἄμβροτος ὁρμή·
αἶψα δὲ θνήτ' ἐφύοντο, τὰ πρὶν μάθον ἀθάνατ' εἶναι,
ζωρά τε τὰ πρὶν, ἄκρητα [κρητά, ?] διαλλάξαντα κε-
      λεύθους.
τῶν δέ τε μισγομένων χεῖτ' ἔθνεα μυρία θνητῶν,
παντοίαις ἰδέηισιν ἀρηρότα, θαῦμα ἰδέσθαι.

But hurrying back, I now will make return
To paths of festal song, laid down before,
Draining each flowing thought from flowing
      thought.
When down the Vortex to the last abyss
Had foundered Hate, and Lovingness had reached
The eddying center of the Mass, behold
Around her into Oneness gathered all.
Yet not a-sudden, but only as willingly
Each from its several region joined with each;

And from their mingling thence are poured abroad
The multitudinous tribes of mortal things.
Yet much unmixed among the mixed remained,
As much as Hate still held in scales, aloft.
For not all blameless did Hate yield and stand
Out yonder on the circle's utmost bounds;
But partwise yet within he stayed, partwise
Was he already from the members gone.
And ever the more skulked away and fled,
Then ever the more, and nearer, inward pressed
The gentle minded, the divine Desire
Of blameless Lovingness. Thence grew apace
Those mortal Things, erstwhile long wont to be
Immortal, and the erstwhile pure and sheer
Were mixed, exchanging highways of new life,
And from their mingling thence are poured abroad
The multitudinous tribes of mortal things,
Knit in all forms and wonderful to see.

36.

τῶν δὲ συνερχομένων ἐξ ἔσχατον ἵστατο Νεῖκος.

And as they came together, Hate began
To take his stand far on the outer verge.

Similia similibus.

37.

αὔξει δὲ χθὼν μὲν σφέτερον δέμας, αἰθέρα δ' αἰθήρ.

And Earth through Earth her figure magnifies,
And Air through Air.

The World as It Now Is.

38.

...εἰ δ' ἄγε τοι λέξω πρῶθ' ἥλικά τ' ἀρχήν,
ἐξ ὧν δῆλ' ἐγένοντο τὰ νῦν ἐσορῶμεν ἅπαντα,
γαῖά τε καὶ πόντος πολυκύμων ἠδ' ὑγρὸς ἀήρ
Τιτὰν ἠδ' αἰθὴρ σφίγγων περὶ κύκλον ἅπαντα.

Come! I will name the like-primeval Four,
Whence rose to sight all things we now behold—
Earth, many-billowed Sea, and the moist Air,
And Aether, the Titan. who binds the globe about.

Earth and Air Not Illimitable.

39.

εἴπερ ἀπείρονα γῆς τε βάθη καὶ δαψιλὸς αἰθήρ,
ὡς διὰ πολλῶν δὴ γλώσσης ῥηθέντα ματαίως
ἐκκέχυται στομάτων, ὀλίγον τοῦ παντὸς ἰδόντων.

If Earth's black deeps were endless, and o'er-full
Were the white Ether, as forsooth some tongues
Have idly prated in the babbling mouths
Of those who little of the All have seen...

Sun and Moon.

40.

ἥλιος ὀξυβελὴς ἠδ' ἰλάειρα σελήνη.

Keen-darting Helios and Selene mild.

41.

ἀλλ' ὁ μὲν ἁλισθεὶς μέγαν οὐρανὸν ἀμφιπολεύει.

But the sun's fires, together gathered, move
Attendant round the mighty space of heaven,

42.

ἀπεστέγασεν δὲ οἱ αὐγάς,
ἔστ' ἂν ἴηι καθύπερθεν, ἀπεσκνίφωσε δὲ γαίης
τόσσον ὅσον τ' εὖρος γλαυκώπιδος ἔπλετο μήνης.

And the sun's beams
The moon, in passing under, covers o'er,
And darkens a bleak tract of earth as large
As is the breadth of her, the silver-eyed.

43.

ὡς αὐγὴ τύψασα σεληναίης κύκλον εὐρύν...

As sunbeam striking on the moon's broad disk.

44.

ἀνταυγεῖ πρὸς Ὄλυμπον ἀταρβήτοισι προσώποις.

Toward Olympos back he darts his beams,
With fearless face.

45.

κυκλοτερὲς περὶ γαῖαν ἐλίσσεται ἀλλότριον φῶς.

Round earth revolves a disk of alien light.

46.

ἅρματος ὡς πέρι χνοίη ἐλίσσεται ἥ τε παρ' ἄκρην.

Even as revolves a chariot's nave, which round
The outmost...

47.

ἀθρεῖ μὲν γὰρ ἄνακτος ἐναντίον ἀγέα κύκλον.

For toward the sacred circle of her lord
She gazes face to face.

48.

νύκτα δὲ γαῖα τίθησιν ὑφισταμένοιο φάεσσι.

But earth makes night for beams of sinking sun.

The Darkling Night.

49.

νυκτὸς ἐρημαίης ἀλαώπιδος...

Of night, the lonely, with her sightless eyes.

Wind and Rain.

50.

Ἶρις δ' ἐκ πελάγους ἄνεμον φέρει ἢ μέγαν ὄμβρον.

Iris from sea brings wind or mighty rain.

Fire.

51.

καρπαλίμως δ' ἀνόπαιον...

And fire sprang upward with a rending speed.

The Volcano.

52.

πολλὰ δ' ἔνερθε οὔδεος πυρὰ καίεται.

And many a fire there burns beneath the ground.

Air.

53.

οὕτω γὰρ συνέκυρσε θέων τοτέ, πολλάκι δ' ἄλλως.

For sometimes so upon its course it met,
And ofttimes otherwise.

Things Passing Strange.

54.

αἰθήρ [δ’ αὖ] μακρῇσι κατὰ χθόνα δύετο ῥίζαις.

In Earth sank Ether with deep-stretching roots.

55.

γῆς ἱδρῶτα θάλασσαν.

Earth's sweat, the sea.

56.

ἅλς ἐπάγη ῥιπῇσιν ἐωσμένος ἠελίοιο.

The salt grew solid, smit by beams of sun.

Strange Creatures of Olden Times.

57.

ἦι πολλαὶ μὲν κόρσαι ἀναύχενες ἐβλάστησαν,
γυμνοὶ δ’ ἐπλάζοντο βραχίονες εὔνιδες ὤμων,
ὄμματά τ’ οἷα ἐπλανᾶτο πενητεύοντα μετώπων.

There budded many a head without a neck,
And arms were roaming, shoulderless and bare,
And eyes that wanted foreheads drifted by.

58.

[...μουνομελῆ ἔτι τὰ γυῖα... ὄντα ἐπλανᾶτο...]

In isolation wandered every limb,
Hither and thither seeing union meet.

59.

αὐτὰρ ἐπεὶ κατὰ μεῖζον ἐμίσγετο δαίμονι δαίμων,
ταῦτά τε συμπίπτεσκον, ὅπηι συνέκυρσεν ἕκαστα,
ἄλλα τε πρὸς τοῖς πολλὰ διηνεκῆ ἐξεγένοντο.

But now as <u>God</u> with <u>God</u> was mingled more,   ?
These members fell together where they met,
And many a birth besides was then begot
In a long line of ever varied life.

60.

εἰλίποδ᾽ ἀκριτόχειρα.

Creatures of countless hands and trailing feet.

61.

πολλὰ μὲν ἀμφιπρόσωπα καὶ ἀμφίστερνα φύεσθαι,
βουγενῆ ἀνδρόπρωιρα, τὰ δ᾽ ἔμπαλιν ἐξανατέλλειν
ἀνδροφυῆ βούκρανα, μεμειγμένα τῆι μὲν ἀπ᾽ ἀνδρῶν
τῆι δὲ γυναικοφυῆ, σκιεροῖς ἠσκημένα γυίοις.

Many were born with twofold brow and breast,
Some with the face of man on bovine stock,
Some with man's form beneath a bovine head,
Mixed shapes of being with shadowed secret parts,
Sometimes like men, and sometimes woman-
    growths.

62.

νῦν δ᾽ ἄγ᾽, ὅπως ἀνδρῶν τε πολυκλαύτων τε γυναικῶν
ἐννυχίους ὅρπηκας ἀνήγαγε κρινόμενον πῦρ,
τῶνδε κλύ᾽· οὐ γὰρ μῦθος ἀπόσκοπος οὐδ᾽ ἀδαήμων.
οὐλοφυεῖς μὲν πρῶτα τύποι χθονὸς ἐξανέτελλον,
ἀμφοτέρων ὕδατός τε καὶ ἴδεος αἶσαν ἔχοντες·

τοὺς μὲν πῦρ ἀνέπεμπε θέλον πρὸς ὁμοῖον ἰκέσθαι,
οὔτε τί πω μελέων ἐρατὸν δέμας ἐμφαίνοντας
οὔτ' ἐνοπὴν οἷόν τ' ἐπιχώριον ἀνδράσι γυῖον.

But come! now hear how 'twas the sundered Fire
Led into life the germs, erst whelmed in night,
Of men and women, the pitied and bewailed;
For 'tis a tale that sees and knows its mark.
First rose mere lumps of earth with rude impress,
That had their shares of Water and of Warm.
These then by Fire (in upward zeal to reach
Its kindred Fire in heaven) were shot aloft,
Albeit not yet had they revealed a form
Of lovely limbs, nor yet a human cry,
Nor secret member, common to the male.

The Process of Human Generation To-day.

63.

ἀλλὰ διέσπασται μελέων φύσις· ἡ μὲν ἐν ἀνδρός...

But separate is the birth of human limbs;
For 'tis in part in man's...

64.

τῶι δ' ἐπὶ καὶ Πόθος εἶσι δι' ὄψιος ἀμμιμνήισκων.

Love-longing comes, reminding him who sees.

65.

ἐν δ' ἐχύθη καθαροῖσι· τὰ μὲν τελέθουσι γυναῖκες,
ψύχεος ἀντιάσαντα, [τὰ δ' ἔμπαλιν ἄρρενα θερμοῦ].

Into clean wombs the seeds are poured, and when
Therein they meet with Cold, the birth is girls;
And boys, when contrariwise they meet with Warm.

66.

[εἰς] σχιστοὺς λειμῶνας ...’Αφροδίτης.

Into the cloven meads of Aphrodite.

67.

ἐν γὰρ θερμοτέρωι τοκὰς ἄρρενος ἔπλετο γαστήρ·
καὶ μέλανες διὰ τοῦτο καὶ ἀνδρωδέστεροι ἄνδρες
καὶ λαχνήεντες μᾶλλον.

For bellies with the warmer wombs become
Mothers of boys, and therefore men are dark,
More stalwart and more shaggy.

68.

μηνὸς ἐν ὀγδοάτου δεκάτηι πύον ἔπλετο λευκόν.

On the tenth day, in month the eighth, the blood
Becomes white pus.

69.

δίγονοι.

Twice bearing.

70.

ἀμνίον.

Sheepskin.

On Animals and Plants.

71.

εἰ δέ τί σοι περὶ τῶνδε λιπόξυλος ἔπλετο πίστις,
πῶς ὕδατος γαίης τε καὶ αἰθέρος ἠελίου τε
κιρναμένων εἴδη τε γενοίατο χροιά τε θνητῶν
τόσσ’, ὅσα νῦν γεγάασι συναρμοσθέντ’ ’Αφροδίτηι...

And if belief lack pith, and thou still doubt
How from the mingling of the elements,
The Earth and Water, the <u>Ether</u> and the Sun, *air*
So many forms and hues of mortal things
Could thus have being, as have come to be,
Each framed and knit by Aphrodite's power...

72.

πῶς καὶ δένδρεα μακρὰ καὶ εἰνάλιοι καμασῆνες...

As the tall trees and fish in briny floods.

73.

ὡς δὲ τότε χθόνα Κύπρις, ἐπεί τ' ἐδίηνεν ἐν ὄμβρωι,
ἴδεα ποιπνύουσα θοῶι πυρὶ δῶκε κρατῦναι...

As Kypris, after watering Earth with Rain,
Zealous to heat her, then did give Earth o'er
To speed of Fire that then she might grow firm.

74.

φῦλον ἄμουσον ἄγουσα πολυσπερέων καμασήνων.

Leading the songless shoals of spawning fish.

75.

τῶν δ' ὅσ' ἔσω μὲν πυκνά, τὰ δ' ἔκτοθι μανὰ πέπηγε,
Κύπριδος ἐν παλάμηισι πλάδης τοιῆσδε τυχόντα...

Of beasts, inside compact with outsides loose,
Which, in the palms of Aphrodite shaped,
Got this their sponginess.

76.

τοῦτο μὲν ἐν κόγχαισι θαλασσονόμων βαρυνώτοις,
ναὶ μὴν κηρύκων τε λιθορρίνων χελύων τε·
ἔνθ’ ὄψει χθόνα χρωτὸς ὑπέρτατα ναιετάουσαν.

’Tis thus with conchs upon the heavy chines
Of ocean-dwellers, aye, of shell-fish wreathed,
Or stony-hided turtles, where thou mark’st
The earthen crust outside the softer parts.

77-78.

[δένδρεα δ’] ἐμπεδόφυλλα καὶ ἐμπεδόκαρπα τέθηλεν
καρπῶν ἀφθονίηισι κατ’ ἠέρα πάντ’ ἐνιαυτόν.

Trees bore perennial fruit, perennial fronds,
Laden with fruit the whole revolving year,
Since fed forever by a fruitful air.

79.

οὕτω δ’ ὠιοτοκεῖ μακρὰ δένδρεα πρῶτον ἐλαίας.

Thus first tall olives lay their yellow eggs.

80.

οὕνεκεν ὀψίγονοί τε σίδαι καὶ ὑπέρφλοια μῆλα.

Wherefore pomegranates slow in ripening be,
And apples grow so plentiful in juice.

81.

οἶνος ἀπὸ φλοιοῦ πέλεται σαπὲν ἐν ξύλωι ὕδωρ.

Wine is but water fermented in the wood,
And issues from the rind.

82.

ταὐτὰ τρίχες καὶ φύλλα καὶ οἰωνῶν πτερὰ πυκνά
καὶ λεπίδες γίγνονται ἐπὶ στιβαροῖσι μέλεσσιν.

From the same stuff on sturdy limbs grow hair,
Leaves, scales of fish, and bird's thick-feathered
plumes.

83.

αὐτὰρ ἐχίνοις
ὀξυβελεῖς χαῖται νώτοις ἐπιπεφρίκασιν.

Stiff hairs, keen-piercing, bristle on the chines
Of hedge-hogs.

Our Eyes.

84.

ὡς δ' ὅτε τις πρόοδον νοέων ὡπλίσσατο λύχνον
χειμερίην διὰ νύκτα, πυρὸς σέλας αἰθομένοιο
ἅψας, παντοίων ἀνέμων λαμπτῆρας ἀμοργούς,
οἵ τ' ἀνέμων μὲν πνεῦμα διασκιδνᾶσιν ἀέντων,
φῶς δ' ἔξω διαθρῶισκον, ὅσον ταναώτερον ἦεν,
λάμπεσκεν κατὰ βηλὸν ἀτειρέσιν ἀκτίνεσσιν·
ὡς δὲ τότ' ἐν μήνιγξιν ἐεργμένον ὠγύγιον πῦρ
λεπτῆισίν [τ'] ὀθόνηισι λοχάζετο κύκλοπα κούρην,
[αἳ] χοάνηισι δίαντα τετρήατο θεσπεσίηισιν·
αἱ δ' ὕδατος μὲν βένθος ἀπέστεγον ἀμφιναέντος,
πῦρ δ' ἔξω δίεσκον, ὅσον ταναώτερον ἦεν.

As when a man, about to sally forth,
Prepares a light and kindles him a blaze
Of flaming fire against the wintry night,
In horny lantern shielding from all winds;

Though it protect from breath of blowing winds,
Its beam darts outward, as more fine and thin,
And with untiring rays lights up the sky:
Just so the Fire primeval once lay hid
In the round pupil of the eye, enclosed
In films and gauzy veils, which through and through
Were pierced with pores divinely fashioned,
And thus kept off the watery deeps around,
Whilst Fire burst outward, as more fine and thin.

85.

ἡ δὲ φλὸξ ἱλάειρα μινυνθαδίης τύχε γαίης.

The gentle flame of eye did chance to get
Only a little of the earthen part.

86.

ἐξ ὧν ὄμματ᾽ ἔπηξεν ἀτειρέα δῖ᾽ Ἀφροδίτη.

From which by Aphrodite, the divine,
The untiring eyes were formed.

87.

γόμφοις ἀσκήσασα καταστόργοις Ἀφροδίτη.

Thus Aphrodite wrought with bolts of love.

88.

μία γίγνεται ἀμφοτέρων ὄψ.

One vision of two eyes is born.

Similia similibus.

89.

γνούς, ὅτι πάντων εἰσὶν ἀπορροαί, ὅσσ' ἐγένοντο...

Knowing that all things have their emanations.

90.

ὡς γλυκὺ μὲν γλυκὺ μάρπτε, πικρὸν δ' ἐπὶ πικρὸν
  ὄρουσεν,
ὀξὺ δ' ἐπ' ὀξὺ ἔβη, δαερὸν δ' ἐποχεῖτο δαηρῶι.

Thus Sweet seized Sweet, Bitter on Bitter flew,
Sour sprung for Sour, and upon Hot rode Hot.

91.

οἴνωι... μᾶλλον ἐνάρθμιον, αὐτὰρ ἐλαίωι
οὐκ ἐθέλει.

Water to wine more nearly is allied,
But will not mix with oil.

92.

τῶι καττιτέρωι μειχθέντα τὸν χαλκόν...

As when one mixes with the copper tin.

93.

βύσσωι δὲ γλαυκῆς κόκκος καταμίσγεται ἀκτῆς.

With flax is mixed the silvery elder's seed.

The Black River Bottoms.

94.

et niger in fundo fluvii color exstat ab umbra,
atque cavernosis itidem spectatur in antris.

And the black color of the river's deeps
Comes all from shade; and one may see the same
In hollow caves.

Eyes.

95.

Κύπριδος ἐν παλάμῃσιν ὅτε ξὺμ πρῶτ᾽ ἐφύοντο.

As, in the palms of Kypris shaped, they first
Began to grow together...

Bones.

96.

ἡ δὲ χθὼν ἐπίηρος ἐν εὐστέρνοις χοάνοισι
τὼ δύο τῶν ὀκτὼ μερέων λάχε Νήστιδος αἴγλης,
τέσσαρα δ᾽ Ἡφαίστοιο· τὰ δ᾽ ὀστέα λευκὰ γένοντο
Ἁρμονίης κόλλῃσιν ἀρηρότα θεσπεσίηθεν.

Kind Earth for her broad-breasted melting-pots,
Of the eight parts got two of Lucid Nestis,
And of Hephæstos four. Thence came white bones,
Divinely joined by glue of Harmony.

97.

ῥάχιν.

The back-bone.

Blood and Flesh.

98.

ἡ δὲ Χθὼν τούτοισιν ἴση συνέκυρσε μάλιστα,
Ἡφαίστωι τ᾽ ὄμβρωι τε καὶ αἰθέρι παμφανόωντι,
Κύπριδος ὁρμισθεῖσα τελείοις ἐν λιμένεσσιν

εἶτ᾽ ὀλίγον μείζων εἴτε πλεόνεσσιν ἐλάσσων·
ἐκ τῶν αἷμά τε γέντο καὶ ἄλλης εἴδεα σαρκός.

And after Earth within the perfect ports
Of Aphrodite anchored lay, she met.
Almost in equal parts Hephæstos red,
And Rain and Ether, the all-splendorous
(Although the parts of Earth were sometimes less,
Sometimes a little more than theirs). From these
There came our blood and all the shapes of flesh.

The Ear.

99.

κώδων. σάρκινος ὄζος.

A bell... a fleshy twig.

The Rushing Blood and the Clepsydra.

100.

ὧδε δ᾽ ἀναπνεῖ πάντα καὶ ἐκπνεῖ· πᾶσι λίφαιμοι
σαρκῶν σύριγγες πύματον κατὰ σῶμα τέτανται,
καί σφιν ἐπὶ στομίοις πυκιναῖς τέτρηνται ἄλοξιν
ῥινῶν ἔσχατα τέρθρα διαμπερές, ὥστε φόνον μέν
κεύθειν, αἰθέρι δ᾽ εὐπορίην διόδοισι τετμῆσθαι.
ἔνθεν ἔπειθ᾽ ὁπόταν μὲν ἀπαΐξῃ τέρεν αἷμα,
αἰθὴρ παφλάζων καταΐσσεται οἴδματι μάργωι,
εὖτε δ᾽ ἀναθρώισκῃ, πάλιν ἐκπνέει, ὥσπερ ὅταν παῖς
κλεψύδρῃ παίζῃσι διειπετέος χαλκοῖο·
εὖτε μὲν αὐλοῦ πορθμὸν ἐπ᾽ εὐειδεῖ χερὶ θεῖσα
εἰς ὕδατος βάπτῃσι τέρεν δέμας ἀργυφέοιο,
οὐδ᾽ ἔτ᾽ ἐς ἄγγοσδ᾽ ὄμβρος ἐσέρχεται, ἀλλά μιν εἴργει
ἀέρος ὄγκος ἔσωθε πεσὼν ἐπὶ τρήματα πυκνά,
εἰσόκ᾽ ἀποστεγάσῃ πυκινὸν ῥόον· αὐτὰρ ἔπειτα

πνεύματος ἐλλείποντος ἐσέρχεται αἴσιμον ὕδωρ.
ὧς δ' αὔτως, ὅθ' ὕδωρ μὲν ἔχηι κάτα βένθεα χαλκοῦ
πορθμοῦ χωσθέντος βροτέωι χροΐ ἠδὲ πόροιο,
αἰθὴρ δ' ἐκτὸς ἔσω λελιημένος ὄμβρον ἐρύκει
ἀμφὶ πύλας ἰσθμοῖο δυσηχέος, ἄκρα κρατύνων,
εἰσόκε χειρὶ μεθῆι· τότε δ' αὖ πάλιν, ἔμπαλιν ἢ πρίν,
πνεύματος ἐμπίπτοντος ὑπεκθέει αἴσιμον ὕδωρ.
ὧς δ' αὔτως τέρεν αἷμα κλαδασσόμενον διὰ γυίων
ὁππότε μὲν παλίνορσον ἀπαΐξειε μυχόνδε,
αἰθέρος εὐθὺς ῥεῦμα κατέρχεται οἴδματι θῦον,
εὖτε δ' ἀναθρώισκηι, πάλιν ἐκπνέει ἴσον ὀπίσσω.

And thus does all breathe in and out. In all,
Over the body's surface, bloodless tubes
Of flesh are stretched, and, at their outlets, rifts
Innumerable along the outmost rind
Are bored; and so the blood remains within;
For air, however, is cut a passage free.
And when from here the thin blood backward
    streams,
The air comes rushing in with roaring swell;
But when again it forward leaps, the air
In turn breathes out; as when a little girl
Plays with a water-clock of gleaming bronze:
As long as ever the opening of the pipe
Is by her pretty fingers stopped and closed,
And thuswise plunged within the yielding mass
Of silvery water, can the Wet no more
Get in the vessel; but the air's own weight,
That falls inside against the countless holes,
Keeps it in check, until the child at last

Uncovers and sets free the thickened air,
When of a truth the water's destined bulk
Gets in, as air gives way. Even so it is,
When in the belly of the brazen clock
The water lies, and the girl's finger tip
Shuts pipe and tube: the air, that from without
Comes pressing inward, holds the water back
About the gateways of the gurgling neck,
As the child keeps possession of the top,
Until her hand will loosen, when amain—
Quite contrariwise to way and wise before—
Pours out and under the water's destined bulk,
As air drops down and in. Even so it is
With the thin blood that through our members
        drives:
When hurrying back it streams to inward, then
Amain a flow of air comes rushing on;
But when again it forward leaps, the air
In turn breathes out along the selfsame way.

Scent.

101.

κέρματα θηρείων μελέων μυκτῆρσιν ἐρευνῶν,
[ζώονθ’] ὅσσ’ ἀπέλειπε ποδῶν ἀπαλῆι περὶ ποίηι ...

Sniffing with nostrils mites from wild beasts' limbs,
Left by their feet along the tender grass. . . .

102.

ὧδε μὲν οὖν πνοιῆς τε λελόγχασι πάντα καὶ ὀσμῶν.

And thus got all things share of breath and smells.

On the Psychic Life.

103.

τῆιδε μὲν οὖν ἰότητι Τύχης πεφρόνηκεν ἅπαντα.

Thus all things think their though by will of Chance.

104.

καὶ καθ' ὅσον μὲν ἀραιότατα ξυνέκυρσε πεσόντα.

And in so far the lightest at their fall
Do strike together....

105.

αἵματος ἐν πελάγεσσι τεθραμμένη ἀντιθορόντος,
τῆι τε νόημα μάλιστα κικλήσκεται ἀνθρώποισιν·
αἷμα γὰρ ἀνθρώποις περικάρδιόν ἐστι νόημα.

In the blood-streams, back-leaping unto it,
The heart is nourished, where prevails the power
That men call thought; for lo the blood that stirs
About the heart is man's controlling thought.

106.

πρὸς παρεὸν γὰρ μῆτις ἀέξεται ἀνθρώποισιν.

For unto men their thrift of reason grows,
According to the body's thrift and state.

107.

ἐκ τούτων [γὰρ] πάντα πεπήγασιν ἁρμοσθέντα
καὶ τούτοις φρονέουσι καὶ ἥδοντ' ἠδ' ἀνιῶνται.

For as of these commingled all things are,
Even so through these men think, rejoice, or grieve.

108.

ὅσσον [δ'] ἀλλοῖοι μετέφυν, τόσον ἄρ σφισιν αἰεί
καὶ τὸ φρονεῖν ἀλλοῖα παρίσταται . . .

As far as mortals change by day, so far
By night their thinking changes...

109.

γαίηι μὲν γὰρ γαῖαν ὀπώπαμεν, ὕδατι δ' ὕδωρ,
αἰθέρι δ' αἰθέρα δῖον, ἀτὰρ πυρὶ πῦρ ἀίδηλον,
στοργὴν δὲ στοργῆι, νεῖκος δέ τε νείκεϊ λυγρῶι.

For 'tis through Earth that Earth we do behold,
Through Ether, divine Ether luminous,
Through Water, Water, through Fire, devouring
    Fire,
And Love through Love, and Hate through doleful
    Hate.

110.

εἰ γὰρ κέν σφ' ἀδινῆισιν ὑπὸ πραπίδεσσιν ἐρείσας
εὐμενέως καθαρῆισιν ἐποπτεύσηις μελέτηισιν,
ταῦτά τέ σοι μάλα πάντα δι' αἰῶνος παρέσονται,
ἄλλα τε πόλλ' ἀπὸ τῶνδ' ἐκτήσεαι· αὐτὰ γὰρ αὔξει
ταῦτ' εἰς ἦθος ἕκαστον, ὅπηι φύσις ἐστὶν ἑκάστωι.
εἰ δὲ σύ γ' ἀλλοίων ἐπορέξεαι, οἷα κατ' ἄνδρας
μυρία δειλὰ πέλονται ἅ τ' ἀμβλύνουσι μερίμνας,
ἦ σ' ἄφαρ ἐκλείψουσι περιπλομένοιο χρόνοιο
σφῶν αὐτῶν ποθέοντα φίλην ἐπὶ γένναν ἱκέσθαι·
πάντα γὰρ ἴσθι φρόνησιν ἔχειν καὶ νώματος αἶσαν.

For if reliant on a spirit firm,
With inclination and endeavor pure,

Thou wilt behold them, all these things shall be
Forever thine, for service, and besides
Thereof full many another shalt thou gain;
For of themselves into that core they grow
Of each man's nature, where his essence lies.
But if for others thou wilt look and reach—
Such empty treasures, myriad and vile,
As men be after, which forevermore
Blunt soul and keen desire—O then shall these
Most swiftly leave thee as the seasons roll;
For all their yearning is a quick return
Unto their own primeval stock. For know:
All things have fixed intent and share of thought.

Dominion.

III.

φάρμακα δ' ὅσσα γεγᾶσι κακῶν καὶ γήραος ἄλκαρ
πεύσῃι, ἐπεὶ μούνωι σοὶ ἐγὼ κρανέω τάδε πάντα.
παύσεις δ' ἀκαμάτων ἀνέμων μένος οἵ τ' ἐπὶ γαῖαν
ὀρνύμενοι πνοιαῖσι καταφθινύθουσιν ἀρούρας·
καὶ πάλιν, ἢν ἐθέλῃσθα, παλίντιτα πνεύματα ἐπάξεις·
θήσεις δ' ἐξ ὄμβροιο κελαινοῦ καίριον αὐχμόν·
ἀνθρώποις, θήσεις δὲ καὶ ἐξ αὐχμοῖο θερείου
ῥεύματα δενδρεόθρεπτα, τά τ' αἰθέρι ναιήσονται,
ἄξεις δ' ἐξ Ἀίδαο καταφθιμένου μένος ἀνδρός.

And thou shalt master every drug that e'er
Was made defense 'gainst sickness and old age—
For thee alone all this I will fulfil—
And thou shalt calm the might of tireless winds,
That burst on earth and ruin seedlands; aye,

And if thou wilt, shalt thou arouse the blasts,
And watch them take their vengeance, wild and
    shrill,
For that before thou cowedst them. Thou shalt
    change
Black rain to drought, at seasons good for men,
And the long drought of summer shalt thou change
To torrents, nourishing the mountain trees,
As down they stream from ether. And thou shalt
From Hades beckon the might of perished men.

THE PURIFICATIONS.

The Healer and Prophet.

112.

ὦ φίλοι, οἳ μέγα ἄστυ κατὰ ξανθοῦ ᾿Ακράγαντος
ναίετ᾿ ἀν᾿ ἄκρα πόλεος, ἀγαθῶν μελεδήμονες ἔργων,
ξείνων αἰδοῖοι λιμένες κακότητος ἄπειροι,
χαίρετ᾿· ἐγὼ δ᾿ ὑμῖν θεὸς ἄμβροτος, οὐκέτι θνητός
πωλεῦμαι μετὰ πᾶσι τετιμένος, ὥσπερ ἔοικα,
ταινίαις τε περίστεπτος στέφεσίν τε θαλείοις·
τοῖσιν ἅμ᾿ [εὖτ᾿] ἂν ἵκωμαι ἐς ἄστεα τηλεθάοντα,
ἀνδράσιν ἠδὲ γυναιξί, σεβίζομαι· οἱ δ᾿ ἅμ᾿ ἕπονται
μυρίοι ἐξερέοντες, ὅπηι πρὸς κέρδος ἀταρπός,
οἱ μὲν μαντοσυνέων κεχρημένοι, οἱ δ᾿ ἐπὶ νούσωι
παντοίων ἐπύθοντο κλύειν εὐηκέα βάξιν
δηρὸν δὴ χαλεποῖσι πεπαρμένοι [ἀμφὶ μόγοισιν].

Ye friends, who in the mighty city dwell
Along the yellow Acragas hard by
The Acropolis, ye stewards of good works,
The stranger's refuge venerable and kind,
All hail, O friends! But unto ye I walk
As god immortal now, no more as man,
On all sides honored fittingly and well,
Crowned both with fillets and with flowering
    wreaths.
When with my throngs of men and women I come

To thriving cities, I am sought by prayers,
And thousands follow me that they may ask
The path to weal and vantage, craving some
For oracles, whilst others seek to hear
A healing word 'gainst many a foul disease
That all too long hath pierced with grievous pains.

113.

ἀλλὰ τί τοῖσδ' ἐπίκειμ' ὡσεὶ μέγα χρῆμά τι πράσσων,
εἰ θνητῶν περίειμι πολυφθερέων ἀνθρώπων;

Yet why urge more, as if forsooth I wrought
Some big affair—do I not far excel
The mortals round me, doomed to many deaths!

114.

ὦ φίλοι, οἶδα μὲν οὕνεκ' ἀληθείη πάρα μύθοις,
οὓς ἐγὼ ἐξερέω· μάλα δ' ἀργαλέη [ἦ] γε τέτυκται
ἀνδράσι καὶ δύσζηλος ἐπὶ φρένα πίστιος ὁρμή.

O friends, I know indeed in these the words
Which I will speak that very truth abides;
But greatly troublous unto men alway
Hath been the emulous struggle of Belief
To reach their bosoms.

Expiation and Metempsychosis.

115.

ἔστιν Ἀνάγκης χρῆμα, θεῶν ψήφισμα παλαιόν,
ἀΐδιον, πλατέεσσι κατεσφρηγισμένον ὅρκοις·
εὖτέ τις ἀμπλακίῃσι φόνωι φίλα γυῖα μιήνηι,
[Νείκεΐ θ'] ὅς κε ἐπίορκον ἁμαρτήσας ἐπομόσσηι,
δαίμονες οἵτε μακραίωνος λελάχασι βίοιο,

τρίς μιν μυρίας ὥρας ἀπὸ μακάρων ἀλάλησθαι,
φυομένους παντοῖα διὰ χρόνου εἴδεα θνητῶν
ἀργαλέας βιότοιο μεταλλάσσοντα κελεύθους.
αἰθέριον μὲν γάρ σφε μένος πόντονδε διώκει,
πόντος δ' ἐς χθονὸς οὖδας ἀπέπτυσε, γαῖα δ' ἐς αὐγὰς
ἠελίου φαέθοντος, ὁ δ' αἰθέρος ἔμβαλε δίναις·
ἄλλος δ' ἐξ ἄλλου δέχεται, στυγέουσι δὲ πάντες.
τῶν καὶ ἐγὼ νῦν εἰμι, φυγάς θεόθεν καὶ ἀλήτης,
Νείκεϊ μαινομένωι πίσυνος.

There is a word of Fate, an old decree
And everlasting of the gods, made fast
With amplest oaths, that whosoe'er of those
Far spirits, with their lot of age-long life,
Do foul their limbs with slaughter in offense,
Or swear forsworn, as failing of their pledge,
Shall wander thrice ten thousand weary years
Far from the Blessed, and be born through time
In various shapes of mortal kind, which change
Ever and ever troublous paths of life:
For now Air hunts them onward to the Sea;
Now the wild Sea disgorges them on Land;
Now Earth will spue toward beams of radiant Sun;
Whence he will toss them back to whirling Air—
Each gets from other what they all abhor.
And in that brood I too am numbered now,
A fugitive and vagabond from heaven,
As one obedient unto raving Strife.

116.

στυγέει δύστλητον Ἀνάγκην.

Charis abhors intolerable Fate.

117.

ἤδη γάρ ποτ᾽ ἐγὼ γενόμην κοῦρός τε κόρη τε
θάμνος τ᾽ οἰωνός τε καὶ ἔξαλος ἔλλοπος ἰχθύς.

For I was once already boy and girl,
Thicket and bird, and mute fish in the waves.

This Earth of Ours.

118.

κλαῦσά τε καὶ κώκυσα ἰδὼν ἀσυνήθεα χῶρον.

I wept and wailed, beholding the strange place.

119.

ἐξ οἵης τιμῆς τε καὶ ὅσσου μήκεος ὄλβου
ὧδε [πεσὼν κατὰ γαῖαν] ἀναστρέφομαι μετὰ θνητοῖς.

From what large honor and what height of bliss
Am I here fallen to move with mortal kind!

This Sky-Roofed World.

120.

ἠλύθομεν τόδ᾽ ὑπ᾽ ἄντρον ὑπόστεγον ...

And then we came unto a roofèd cave.

This Vale of Tears.

121.

ἀτερπέα χῶρον,
ἔνθα Φόνος τε Κότος τε καὶ ἄλλων ἔθνεα Κηρῶν
αὐχμηραί τε νόσοι καὶ σήψιες ἔργα τε ῥευστά
Ἄτης ἀν λειμῶνα κατὰ σκότος ἠλάσκουσιν.

A joyless land,
Where Slaughter and Grudge, and troops of Dooms
besides,

Where shriveled Diseases and obscene Decays,
And Labors, burdened with the water-jars,
Do wander down the dismal meads of Bane.

122.

ἔνθ᾽ ἦσαν Χθονίη τε καὶ Ἡλιόπη ταναῶπις,
Δῆρίς θ᾽ αἱματόεσσα καὶ Ἁρμονίη θεμερῶπις,
Καλλιστώ τ᾽ Αἰσχρή τε, Θόωσά τε Δηναίη τε,
Νημερτής τ᾽ ἐρόεσσα μελάγκουρός τ᾽ Ἀσάφεια.

There was Earth-mother,
There the far-peering Virgin of the Sun,
And bloody Quarrel and grave-eyed Harmony,
And there was Fair and Foul and Speed and Late,
Black-haired Confusion and sweet maiden Sure.

123.

Φυσώ τε Φθιμένη τε, καὶ Εὐναίη καὶ Ἔγερσις,
Κινώ τ᾽ Ἀστεμφής τε, πολυστέφανός τε Μεγιστώ
καὶ Φορύη, Σωπή τε καὶ Ὀμφαίη ...

Growth and Decay, and Sleep and Roused-from-
    sleep,
Action and Rest, and Glory many-crowned,
And Filth, and Silence and prevailing Voice.

124.

ὢ πόποι, ὢ δειλὸν θνητῶν γένος, ὢ δυσάνολβον,
τοίων ἔκ τ᾽ ἐρίδων ἔκ τε στοναχῶν ἐγένεσθε.

O mortal kind! O ye poor sons of grief!
From such contentions and such sighings sprung!

The Changing Forms.

125.

ἐκ μὲν γὰρ ζωῶν ἐτίθει νεκρὰ εἴδε᾽ ἀμείβων.

For from the living he the dead did make,
Their forms exchanging...

126.

σαρκῶν ἀλλογνῶτι περιστέλλουσα χιτῶνι.

All things doth Nature change, enwrapping souls
In unfamiliar tunics of the flesh.

127.

ἐν θήρεσσι λέοντες ὀρειλεχέες χαμαιεῦναι
γίγνονται, δάφναι δ᾽ ἐνὶ δένδρεσιν ἠυκόμοισιν.

The worthiest dwellings for the souls of men,
When 'tis their lot to live in forms of brutes,
Are tawny lions, those great beasts that sleep
Couched on the black earth up the mountain side;
But, when in forms of beautiful plumed trees
They live, the bays are worthiest for souls.

The Golden Age.

128.

οὐδέ τις ἦν κείνοισιν Ἄρης θεὸς οὐδὲ Κυδοιμός
οὐδὲ Ζεὺς βασιλεὺς οὐδὲ Κρόνος οὐδὲ Ποσειδῶν,
ἀλλὰ Κύπρις βασίλεια.
τὴν οἵ γ᾽ εὐσεβέεσσιν ἀγάλμασιν ἱλάσκοντο
γραπτοῖς τε ζώιοισι μύροισί τε δαιδαλεόδμοις
σμύρνης τ᾽ ἀκρήτου θυσίαις λιβάνου τε θυώδους,
ξουθῶν τε σπονδὰς μελιτῶν ῥίπτοντες ἐς οὖδας·

ταύρων δ' ἀκρήτοισι φόνοις οὐ δεύετο βωμός,
ἀλλὰ μύσος τοῦτ' ἔσκεν ἐν ἀνθρώποισι μέγιστον,
θυμὸν ἀπορραίσαντας ἐνέδμεναι ἠέα γυῖα.

Nor unto them
Was any Ares god, nor Kydoimos,
Nor Zeus, the king of gods, nor Kronos, nor
Poseidon then, but only Kypris queen...
Whom they with holy gifts were wont to appease,
With painted images of living things,
With costly unguents of rich fragrancy,
With gentle sacrifice of taintless myrrh,
With redolent fumes of frankincense, of old
Pouring libations out upon the ground
Of yellow honey; not then with unmixed blood
Of many bulls was ever an altar stained;
But among men 'twas sacrilege most vile
To reave of life and eat the goodly limbs.

The Sage.

129.

ἦν δέ τις ἐν κείνοισιν ἀνὴρ περιώσια εἰδώς,
ὃς δὴ μήκιστον πραπίδων ἐκτήσατο πλοῦτον
παντοίων τε μάλιστα σοφῶν ἐπιήρανος ἔργων·
ὁππότε γὰρ πάσῃσιν ὀρέξαιτο πραπίδεσσιν,
ῥεῖ᾽ ὅ γε τῶν ὄντων πάντων λεύσσεσκεν ἕκαστον
καί τε δέκ᾽ ἀνθρώπων καί τ᾽ εἴκοσιν αἰώνεσσιν.

Was one among them there, a supreme man
Of vastest knowledge, gainer of large wealth
Of understanding, and chief master wise
Of diverse works of skill and wisdom all;

For whensoe'er he sought with scope and reach
Of understanding, then 'twas his to view
Readily each and every thing that e'er
In ten or twenty human ages throve.

Those Days.

130.

ἦσαν δὲ κτίλα πάντα καὶ ἀνθρώποισι προσηνῆ,
θῆρές τ' οἰωνοί τε, φιλοφροσύνη τε δεδήει.

All things were tame, and gentle toward men,
All beasts and birds, and friendship's flame blew
    fair.

The Divine.

131.

εἰ γὰρ ἐφημερίων ἕνεκέν τινος, ἄμβροτε Μοῦσα,
ἡμετέρας μελέτας [μέλε τοι] διὰ φροντίδος ἐλθεῖν,
εὐχομένωι νῦν αὖτε παρίστασο, Καλλιόπεια,
ἀμφὶ θεῶν μακάρων ἀγαθὸν λόγον ἐμφαίνοντι.

For since, O Muse undying, thou couldst deign
To give for these our paltry human cares
A gateway to thy soul, O now much more,
Kalliope of the beautiful dear voice,
Be near me now beseeching!—whilst I speak
Excelling thoughts about the blessed gods.

132.

ὄλβιος, ὃς θείων πραπίδων ἐκτήσατο πλοῦτον,
δειλὸς δ', ὧι σκοτόεσσα θεῶν πέρι δόξα μέμηλεν.

O well with him who hath secured his wealth

Of thoughts divine, O wretched he whose care
Is shadowy speculation on the gods!

133.

οὐκ ἔστιν πελάσασθαι ἐν ὀφθαλμοῖσιν ἐφικτόν
ἡμετέροις ἢ χερσὶ λαβεῖν, ᾗπέρ τε μεγίστη
πειθοῦς ἀνθρώποισιν ἁμαξιτὸς εἰς φρένα πίπτει.

We may not bring It near us with our eyes,
We may not grasp It with our human hands,
With neither hands nor eyes, those highways twain
Whereby Belief drops into minds of men.

134.

οὐδὲ γὰρ ἀνδρομέηι κεφαλῆι κατὰ γυῖα κέκασται,
οὐ μὲν ἀπαὶ νώτοιο δύο κλάδοι ἀίσσονται,
οὐ πόδες, οὐ θοὰ γοῦνα, οὐ μήδεα λαχνήεντα,
ἀλλὰ φρὴν ἱερὴ καὶ ἀθέσφατος ἔπλετο μοῦνον,
φροντίσι κόσμον ἅπαντα καταΐσσουσα θοῆισιν.

For 'tis adorned with never a manlike head,
For from Its back there swing no branching arms,
It hath no feet nor knees alert, nor form
Of tufted secret member; but It lives,
One holy mind, ineffable, alone,
And with swift thoughts darts through the universe.

135.

ἀλλὰ τὸ μὲν πάντων νόμιμον διά τ' εὐρυμέδοντος
αἰθέρος ἠνεκέως τέταται διά τ' ἀπλέτου αὐγῆς.

But the wide law of all extends throughout
Broad-ruling ether and the vast white sky.

Animal Sacrifice.

136.

οὐ παύσεσθε φόνοιο δυσηχέος; οὐκ ἐσορᾶτε
ἀλλήλους δάπτοντες ἀκηδείῃσι νόοιο;

Will ye not cease from this great din of slaughter?
Will ye not see, unthinking as ye are,
How ye rend one another unbeknown?

137.

μορφὴν δ' ἀλλάξαντα πατὴρ φίλον υἱὸν ἀείρας
σφάζει ἐπευχόμενος μέγα νήπιος· οἱ δ' ἐπορεῦνται
λισσόμενοι θύοντας, ὁ δ' αὖ νήκουστος ὁμοκλέων
σφάξας ἐν μεγάροισι κακὴν ἀλεγύνατο δαῖτα.
ὡς δ' αὔτως πατέρ' υἱὸς ἑλὼν καὶ μητέρα παῖδες
θυμὸν ἀπορραίσαντε φίλας κατὰ σάρκας ἔδουσιν.

The father lifteth for the stroke of death
His own dear son within a changèd form,
And slits his throat for sacrifice with prayers—
A blinded fool! But the poor victims press,
Imploring their destroyers. Yet not one
But still is deaf to piteous moan and wail.
Each slits the throat and in his halls prepares
A horrible repast. Thus too the son
Seizes the father, children the mother seize,
And reave of life and eath their own dear flesh.

138.

χαλκῶι ἀπὸ ψυχὴν ἀρύσας

Drawing the soul as water with the bronze.

139.

οἴμ' ὅτι οὐ πρόσθεν με διώλεσε νηλεὲς ἦμαρ,
πρὶν σχέτλι' ἔργα βορᾶς περὶ χείλεσι μητίσασθαι.

Ah woe is me! that never a pitiless day
Destroyed me long ago, ere yet my lips
Did meditate this feeding's monstrous crime!

Taboos.

140.

δάφνης [Φοιβείων] φύλλων ἄπο πάμπαν ἔχεσθαι.

Withhold your hands from leaves of Phœbus' tree!

141.

δειλοί, πάνδειλοι, κυάμων ἄπο χεῖρας ἔχεσθαι.

Ye wretched, O ye altogether wretched,
Your hands from beans withhold!

Sin.

142.

τὸν δ' οὔτ' ἄρ τε Διὸς τέγεοι δόμοι αἰγιόχοιο
τέ[ρποι] ἂν οὐδὲ [αἰνῆς 'Ε]κ[άτ]ης τέγος [ἠλιτό-
ποινον].

Neither roofed halls of ægis-holding Zeus
Delight it, nor dire Hecate's venging house.

143.

κρηνάων ἄπο πέντε ταμόντ' [ἐν] ἀτειρέι χαλκῶι...

Scooping from fountains five with lasting bronze.

144.

νηστεῦσαι κακότητος.

O fast from evil-doing.

145.

τοιγάρτοι χαλεπῆισιν ἀλύοντες κακότησιν
οὔποτε δειλαίων ἀχέων λωφήσετε θυμόν.

Since wildered by your evil-doings huge,
Ne'er shall ye free your life from heavy pains.

The Progression of Rebirth.

146.

εἰς δὲ τέλος μάντεις τε καὶ ὑμνοπόλοι καὶ ἰητροί
καὶ πρόμοι ἀνθρώποισιν ἐπιχθονίοισι πέλονται.
ἔνθεν ἀναβλαστοῦσι θεοὶ τιμῆισι φέριστοι.

And seers at last, and singers of high hymns,
Physicians sage, and chiefs o'er earth-born men
Shall they become, whence germinate the gods,
The excellent in honors.

147.

ἀθανάτοις ἄλλοισιν ὁμέστιοι αὐτοτράπεζοι,
εὔνιες ἀνδρείων ἀχέων, ἀπόκληροι, ἀτειρεῖς.

At hearth and feast companioned with the immor-
tals,
From human pains and wasting eld immune.

Last Echoes of a Song Half Lost.

148.

ἀμφιβρότην χθόνα.

Man-enfolding Earth.

149.

νεφεληγερέτην.

The cloud-collecting.

150.

πολυαίματον ἧπαρ.

The blood-full liver.

151.

ζείδωρος.

Life-giving.

152.

γῆρας ἡμέρας.

Evening, the day's old age.

153.

βαυβώ.

The belly.

153a.

ἐν ἑπτὰ ἑβδομάσιν.

In seven times seven days.

NOTES.

ON NATURE.

Fr. 1. Pausanias is the friend to whom Empedocles addresses himself throughout the poem *On Nature.* Matthew Arnold has made him a character in *Empedocles on Aetna.*

Fr. 2. *Narrow ways*: these are the pores (πόροι) into which pass the emanations (ἀπόρροαι) from things (cf. fr. 89); whence man's portion—such as it is—of perception and knowledge (cf. the simulacra of Lucr. IV). "Ways" (παλάμαι) are literally "devices"; but the notion of small passages is suggested by στεινωποί; cf. fr. 4.

Their little share of life: a note of sadness struck more than once by Empedocles, and one of the few elements in common with the personage in Arnold's poem. Cf. the comments on life and man in the Gnomic writers.

Like smoke: cf.

> "Ergo dissolui quoque convenit omnem animai
> naturam, ceu fumus, in altas aëris auras."
> Lucr., III, 455-6.

Than mortal ken may span: more literally, "than mortal skill may have power to move" (ὄρωρεν).

Fr. 3. Addressed to Pausanias; so elsewhere.

Fr. 4. *Their madness*: this evidently refers to the over-bold speculations of Parmenides and other philosophers.

Meek Piety's: lit., "from [the realm of] Piety."

By every way of knowing: by every passage, or device (παλάμη); cf. fr. 2. Empedocles, unlike Parmenides, affirms the relative trustworthiness of the senses.

Trust sight no more than hearing, etc.: here E. may imply a distinction between the understanding and sense perception;

or he may consider, with the sensationalists of modern psychology, one sense as acting as a check on another, without realizing that there must still be something over and above them which weighs and decides. His theory of knowledge was apparently little developed. Aristotle (*De an.*, III, 3, 427a 21-29) says that E. drew no distinction between νοεῖν or φρονεῖν and αἰσθάνεσθαι.

Note by all ways: "ways" here translates πόρος, 'road,' 'pore.'

The Roman critic (Hor., *De arte poetica*, 134 ff.) warns the poet against a beginning that promises bigger things than the work bears out, and he might have chided Empedocles with the contrary fault; for the reverent attitude, reflected in this fragment, soon gives way to dogmatism and grandiloquence, as the old philosopher's soul thrills to his large thought and the roll of his splendid verse. Later writers on the Unknowable and the limitations of human knowledge have not always been more consistent.

Fr. 5. *The High and Strong*: "either philosophers or doctrines or the gods Love and Strife." Diels, PPF.

Sifted through thy soul: an illustration of the dependence of a poetic value on an emendation; if, instead of διασσηθέντος (FV), we read διατμηθέντος (PPF), the translation might run:

"Deep in thine inward parts dividing thought," a very different, and to me less effective figure.

Fr. 6. *The four-fold root*: the four elements, but there is some disagreement as to the interpretation of the symbols that follow. Nestis is presumably a Sicilian water divinity, identified by van ten Brink and Heyne with Proserpina, and the context shows that she symbolizes water. Zeller (p. 759) makes Zeus fire, Here air, and Aidoneus (Dis) earth; Burnet (p. 243) and Bodrero (p. 78), following Knatz, make Zeus air, Here earth, and Aidoneus fire. I am not persuaded that any peculiar theory is implied in this mythology, as Bodrero attempts to prove (cf. also Gomperz, p. 245); at the most E. is hinting at the elements as eternal (the "established gods" of fr. 17) and primary—"the four-fold root of all things." Moreover, E. was poet no less than philosopher.

Earlier philosophy had recognized the materials which E. calls the four elements, though it had never made them *Grundstoffe*. Cf. also the "flowing" (like water), the "mistiform" (like air) and the dry mist (like fire) of Heraclitus; and the contrasted warm and cold which Anaximander conceived as differentiated from the ἄπειρον. (The five-fold division of Philolaos was probably derived from E.) E. was the first absolute pluralist; preceding thinkers, Thales, Pythagoras, Heraclitus, Parmenides, etc., had made ultimate reality a material One. Not until Plato have we an approach to an idealistic monism (cf. Burnet, p. 207-8).

Fr. 7. *Elements* (στοιχεῖα), supplied here and elsewhere, is nowhere preserved to us by E., and was apparently first used in philosophy by Plato. Cf. Zeller, p. 759.

Fr. 8. *End in ruinous death*: this is not here enlarged upon as is the idea of birth; it is, however, but the other aspect of the latter: the interchange of the mixed implies a scattering as well, the dissolution of the old to form the new; at least I take it so. Cf. fr. 17.

Fr. 9. *In man,* etc.: properly, "in the case of man."

I too assent to use: how many philosophers have felt themselves balked in the perfect expression of their thought by having in their vocabulary to "assent to use."

Fr. 10. *Avenging Death*: evidently used in a connection similar to "doom of death" in fr. 9 (cf. Plut. quoted by Diels, PPF). "ut 'Αθηνᾶ ἀλοῖτις Lycoph. 935 est *sceleris vindex*, sic Mors peccatorum ultrix." Diels, PPF.

Fr. 11-12. The doctrine (and in part the words) of Parmenides, afterwards developed with such energy and imagination and observation of the processes of the sensible universe in Book I of the *De Natura Rerum*.

For there 'twill be, etc.: perhaps a more literal rendering would make the meaning more obvious to some readers: "For every time will it [i. e., any given object] be right there, where any one every time puts it."

Fr. 13-14. E. held with Parmenides that the world is a Plenum, incapable either of excess or of deficiency.

Fr. 15. "But that there is here any affirmation of the immortality of the psychic life (Siebeck, *Gesch. d. Psychol.,* I, 53, 267) I do not believe. βροτοί denotes with E. not only men but all per-

ishable beings, and these are eternal only in so far as their
elements are eternal." Zeller, p. 756.

Diels, however, renders (FV) βροτοί "wir Sterbliche"; indeed, as "men" is evidently the understood subject of καλέουσι
('call'), it must also be the subject of βιῶσι ('live'), and it is
but natural to construe βροτοί below in the same sense. But
there is still presumably no reference to the immortality of the
soul. Thought and feeling with E. are part of the physical
system; and "our being" is but a physical being, to which,
however, as to every thing, the thought of fr. 11 must apply.
"Compacted" and "loosed apart" refer to the mingling and
the scattering of the body's constituent elements.

Fr. 16. *Love and Hate*: under varying names, "Lovingness"
and "Strife," "Aphrodite" and "Wrath," etc., conceived by E.
as the dynamic powers of the universe. Many details of the
conception are still in dispute (cf. Zeller, p. 771; Tannery, p.
306). Efforts to relate them genetically to the Isis and Typhon
of the Egyptian, or to the Ormuzd and Ahriman of the Persian
seem to me unsuccessful; one is rather reminded of the "War"
and "Harmonia" of Heraclitus.

Fr. 17. The longest, the most significant, and the most difficult of
the fragments; preserved by Simplicius. "The One" is the
Sphere; "the Many," as we see from line 18 (of the Greek
text), are the four elements.

Two-fold the birth, two-fold the death of things: a dark
saying; I paraphrase a Latin note of Diels, PPF:

"The wheel of nature runs a double course, one from the
complete separation of the four elements to the union of the
Sphere, the other from the Sphere to the separation of the
elements. In either course exist the certainties of creation
and dissolution: for, as the elements come together, their
meeting (σύνοδος) brings things to birth, but when the tendency to mingle has finally increased so far as to form the
Sphere again, the same meeting is found at last to be no less
the source of their destruction (thus σύνοδος τίκτει τ' ὀλέκει τε);
again, as the elements begin to separate from the Sphere (διαφυομένων), things are born into an orderly arrangement of
their elements, until, with the increased tendency toward separation, everything at last flies apart (διέπτη) and perishes."
Cf. fr. 26.

It must be noted that, when Love is supreme, we have the harmony of the Sphere; when Hate is supreme, a complete dissipation. In neither state is anything like our world possible: we must be in either one or the other intermediate period, where the elements are making headway (1) away from the Sphere toward dissipation, or (2) from dissipation toward the Sphere. Cf. Burnet (p. 248 ff.), who believes we are in the former period.

Anaximander (but cf. Burnet, p. 64) and Heraclitus and the Pythagoreans seem also to have taught a succession of worlds born and destroyed; and a similar thought is implicit in the nebular hypothesis of modern astronomy.

So far have they a birth, etc.: "they" refers, I believe, to the four elements: mortal, if viewed as parts of the perishable things of our world; immortal and unshaken as gods (cf. the mythological names of fr. 6), if viewed as the primeval sources of all things and as subject to the law of the four cosmic periods—eternal interchange and revolution round "the circle of the world."

And shut from them apart, etc.: both Strife and Love are apparently conceived as material, not simply as dynamic principles. The early philosophers were a long way from the incorporealities and abstractions of modern science (cf. Burnet, p. 246); and even the Pythagorean numbers were by no means sharply distinguished from their concrete expression in geometrical forms and material things, and even the "Nous" of Anaxagoras was mindstuff in space. Thus Strife is in equipoise, i. e., everywhere of the same weight (ἀτάλαντον s'entend de l'équilibre des poids. Tannery, p. 305), and at this moment somewhere *outside* the Sphere; while Love, equal in length and breadth, is situated *inside*, and

> "speeds revolving in the elements."

Tannery (p. 306) regards them as "media endowed with special properties and able to displace each other, media in the bosom of which are plunged the corporeal molecules, but which are still conceived to be as material as the imponderable ether of the modern physicists," i. e., almost as diffused gases; but it is very doubtful if Empedocles had such a definite thought in mind.

'Tis she inborn, etc.: whatever the difficulties in thinking out the thought with consistency of detail, there is a freshness

and a grandeur in this identification of a cosmic principle, or material, with a passion, or a faculty, in the life of man. E. makes a similar identification of Hate (cf. fr. 109). Schopenhauer's identification of the dynamic principle of all nature with "will" offers a modern analogy. Nor should we overlook the prior significance in the very choice of the names, drawn from the passions of men to stand for activities as fundamental and wide as the universe.

I think, by the way, that E.'s language here makes it possible to interpret love ("thoughts of love," etc.) as more than the physiological passion of sex for sex, with which it is usually identified by the commentators.

Behold these elements own equal strength, etc.: E. conceives the elements as each alike in quantity and strength, each alike primeval; but each, with its peculiar function and appearance (cf. E's specific descriptive adjectives used in naming the elements), qualitatively distinct from the others. Cf. Zeller, p. 762. But what he means by affirming that

"each
Prevailing conquers with revolving time"

is not, to me at least, perfectly clear. He speaks nowhere of an age of Air, or Earth, or Water; and the peculiar agencies he imputes to fire (see infra) are apparently at all times at work, without ever ending in fire's dominating all, as in the common interpretation of the system of Heraclitus. Possibly he refers to the temporal sequence in the separation of the elements from the Sphere (for which see Zeller, p. 787), or simply to the fact that now this, now that created object in natura rerum has more of this or more of that element in its composition. Cf. fr. 26. In Chinese philosophy "The elements are supposed to conquer one another according to a definite law. We are told that wood conquers earth, earth conquers water, water conquers fire, fire conquers metal, and metal conquers wood." Paul Carus, *Chinese Thought*, 1907, p. 47. But there is nothing in E.'s thought that seems to correspond.

Through one another: an allusion to the theory of the pores, the precursor of Atomism. Cf. Zeller, p. 767.

Fr. 18. The translator has made no effort to be consistent in rendering φιλίη and φιλότης into English by different words. There is evidently no vital difference of meaning in the Greek as used by E. Cf. Plut., quoted by Diels, PPF.

Fr. 19. With reference here to water.

Fr. 20. Line 1 has been supplied by the translator. Cf. with this fragment fr. 57-62.

Fr. 21. *But come*, etc.: i. e., 'observe if what I have already said does not give a sufficiently clear description of the form, or physical characteristics of the elements'—"si quid materiae etiam in priore numeratione elementorum relictum erat formae explicandae." Diels, PPF.

The Sun: see note on fr. 41.

The eternal Stars: E. conceived the fixed stars as fastened to the vault (of the dark hemisphere), the planets as free, and both as formed of fire separated from the air.

The sun and the stars apparently correspond to the fiery element, rain to the watery, and earth to the earthy, considered here as visible parts of the present universe no less than as the sources thereof. Air seems to be unrepresented, unless it be suggested by "glowing radiance." I am inclined to take the phrase merely as a bit of poetry—it is the radiance of the night, hardly the bright heaven, the aery expanse of day. But were it so interpreted, one might well note that E. regularly uses αἰθήρ ('sky') and once οὐρανός ('heaven') for air, and might compare Lucretius'

"Unde aether sidera pascit" (Bk. I, 231),

and Virgil's

"Polus dum sidera pascit" (Bk. I, 608)—

phrases which, however, are not, as I understand them, based on an astronomy like that of Empedocles.

The green: the Greek is θέλυμνα, 'the beginnings of things,' the 'semina rerum' of Lucretius (Liddell & Scott), here possibly with some suggestion of the growth of the vegetable world (hence the translation "green"). There is assuredly no reference to the primeval "lumps with rude impress" of fr. 62, for E. is here speaking of things as they *are*.

The long-lived gods: the gods in the *On Nature* of Empedocles are part of the perishable world, formed, like tree or fish, out of the elements; hence, though "in honors excellent," they are not immortal.

Fr. 22. *Heaven*: air; cf. note to fr. 21.

For amber Sun, etc.: the mutual attraction of the like and
the repulsion of the unlike are here referred respectively to
the action of Love and Hate; but elsewhere in his system Empedocles leaves us much in the dark on the matter. Cf. Gomperz, p. 237. Tannery, p. 308. Also Burnet, p. 247.

Things that are most apt to mix: where the emanations of
the one are peculiarly well fitted to the pores of the other. Cf.
Burnet, 247 ff.

Fr. 23. *mixing harmonious,* etc.: Gomperz (p. 233) sees a reference in
this fragment to the four primary colors, as analogous to the
four elements. The simile were then doubly striking.

The goddess: lit., 'divinity' (θεοῦ), undoubtedly the Muse,
mentioned several times by E. (cf. fr. 4, 5, 131); important
as a hint that the author is poet as well as philosopher, and
may use language not always literally in accord with his system.

Fr. 25. One may regret that Empedocles has not left us more such
pithy sayings.

Cf.

"A reasonable reason,
If good, is none the worse for repetition."
Byron, *Don Juan,* XV, 51.

Fr. 26. *In turn they conquer*: "they" means the elements; cf. note
on fr. 17.

olden Fate: fate is mentioned several times by E., and can
only mean, I think, the universal law of being.

Whiles in fair order: Gr. εἰς ἕνα κόσμον; it refers to that
orderly arrangement of the elements which results, as the uni-
fying process goes on, in the dead harmony of the Sphere.

Whiles rent asunder: this refers to the process which ends
in the complete dissipation of the elements and the destruction
of all things.

Till they, when grown....succumb: i. e., as I understand it,
till, after having completed the process of coming together
again which ends in the Sphere, they again begin the process
of separating which ends in dissipation. Cf. fr. 17; and Zeller
(p. 778), who might question this interpretation.

"Go under and succumb" is in the Greek ὑπένερθε γένηται, a phrase found in Theognis (1. 843):

" 'Αλλ' ὁπόταν καθύπερθεν ἐὼν ὑπένερθε γένηται,
τουτάκις οἴκαδ' ἴμεν παυσάμενοι πόσιος,"

where the event is, however, hardly of the same cosmic importance.

Fr. 27.   *There*: in the Sphere, where one could distinguish none of the elements and none of the forms of things. One notes that the passage makes no mention of air, and wonders if a line may have been lost. The Sphere corresponds somewhat to the "Being" of Parmenides, which was spherical and immovable; but the four elements, though in this sphere visibly indistinguishable, must still maintain their respective qualities. For various ancient interpretations of the nature of the Sphere, cf. Burnet, p. 250 ff.

In the close recess of Harmony: "in Concordiae latebris fixus tenetur." Diels, PPF. A poetic figure for the idea that the Sphere is completely under the reign of Love. Possibly "the close recess" is but the "surrounding solitude" below, and is not, perhaps, to be taken any more literally than the reference to the Sphere as "exultant." If examined narrowly, however, difficulties must be admitted. The figure may be Pythagorean. Harmony, then, were the personified "fitting," "adaptation," and would refer to the closely fitted parts of the universe, when brought together by Love. Πύκινος ('close-fitted,' 'compact') were itself perfectly appropriate; but κρύφος, as a noun (meaning, as it seems to here, 'a hidden place') would confuse the thought, for the figure, if Pythagorean, requires us to conceive "Harmony" as pervading the Sphere, not as hiding it somewhere in space. Moreover, one would expect to find κρύφος applied to the Sphere rather than to the recess. Prof. Newbold in a letter suggests κρύῳ for κρύφῳ, i. e., 'in Harmonia's close-binding *frost*,' as "better than the MS reading, though not altogether satisfactory."

Bodrero assumes (p. 135) that Harmony "is not Love alone, but the union of Love and Hate, their equilibrium"; but his whole interpretation of Empedocles is very far from that of all other scholars, and is usually, as here, of little service to the point of view adopted in these pages.

The rounded Sphere: This primeval Sphere must never be confounded with E.'s present spherical universe, composed, as we learn from the doxographers, of a revolving bright hemisphere of day and a dark hemisphere of night. Cf. note to fr. 48.

Exultant in surrounding solitude: quoted with literary tact, though in a corrupt form, by Marcus Aurelius (XII, 3): "If thou wilt separate, I say, from this ruling faculty the things which are attached to it by the impressions of sense, and the things of time to come and of time that is past, and wilt make thyself like Empedocles' Sphere, 'All round, and in its joyous rest reposing.'"

Fr. 29. Cf. fr. 134, where expressions, in part identical, are used apparently of the Divine; and note that below in fr. 31 the Sphere is called God.

Nor form of life-producing member: a touch possible only to a free and an austere imagination: Empedocles gazes upon man, the naked and the swift, and seizes at once on that which most identifies his manhood.

Fr. 30. *Yet after mighty Strife*: it will be remembered that Strife breaks up and separates the elements in the Sphere.

Amplest oath: Gr. πλατέος ὅρκου, lit. 'broad oath.' Cf. fr. 115.

Fr. 31. *God*: the Sphere. "This mixture of all materials is divine only in the sense in which antiquity in general sees in the world itself the totality of divine beings and powers." Zeller, p. 813; cf. p. 814.

Fr. 32. "quod e coniectura scripsi *artus iungit bina* eleganter expressit Martianus Rota sive ingenio sive meliore libro fretus: *articulis constat semper iunctura duobus.*" Diels, PPF.

Fr. 33. Diels (PPF) cites Homer, E, 902, and says "e Plut. patet Concordiæ processum illustrari"—it illustrates the process of Love.

Fr. 34. i. e., like a baker, according to Karsten and Burnet.

Fr. 35. *When down the Vortex*: the origin of the vortex is not explained in any existing fragment of Empedocles. Tannery thinks (p. 312) "the vortex is due to a disturbance of equilibrium....the final resultant of the disordered movements which Hate occasions in the Sphere." And again (p. 314): "Hate....is the principle of division and movement; in consequence of its very mobility it works its way naturally into the interior of the motionless Sphere, produces an agitation and then a movement of revolution. Thereupon Hate is thrown off to the circumference where the movement is most rapid, and is finally excluded altogether." But cf. Zeller, p. 784, 787. This chaos, or vortex, caused, according to Tannery by Hate, has suggested to some the "χάσμα" of Hesiod and the "rudes indigestaque moles" of Ovid; it was, however, an accepted tenet of the older schools (cf. *The δίνη in Anaximenes and Anaximander*, W. A. Heidel, *Class. Philology*, I, 3., July 1906).

The eddying centre of the mass: "the mass" is not in the Greek; but is to be understood rather than "the Sphere"— which has properly ceased to be in becoming a vortex.

Oneness: not to be identified with the Sphere, but with the "fair order" of fr. 26, as seems clear from the lines that follow, "and from their mingling," etc.

Only as willingly: possibly a reference to the attraction of like for like. Cf. note to fr. 22.

Not all blameless: i. e., Hate retreated under protest, differing from "blameless Lovingness" in not willingly submitting to the "old decree" (see Diels, PPF, and fr. 30); although this seems, if anything more than a poetic touch, to involve the inconsistency of a free will over against the fundamental necessity. Such cruxes recall the inconsistencies even in the more developed materialism of modern times, which assumes the possibility of sense experience and of distinguishing truth and error, right and wrong. Cf. fr. 116.

The circle's utmost bounds: the circumference of the vortex, not the Sphere.

The members: the elements.

Those mortal things: the elements as constituents of physical objects in the perishable world, contrasted with the elements as eternal sources of creation. Cf. fr. 17 and 26. "Dagli elementi eterni si formano esseri viventi e peribili." Bodrero, p. 130. The two states are again contrasted in

> "The erstwhile pure and sheer
> Were mixed,"

below.

Fr. 36. *They*: The elements. Cf. preceding fragment.

Fr. 37. "cetera elementa duo commemorata fuisse veri simile (cf.
Lucr. II 1114 sq.), at versus recuperari nequit." Diels, PPF.
Cf. fr. 109 on sense perception.

Fr. 38. If the brief examples of "all things we now behold" are to
correspond to the four elements, one finds nothing representa-
tive of fire, unless ether be here used, as by Anaxagoras, for
fire, with reference to the fiery sky (cf. note to fr. 135) and
to the etymology of the word itself (from αἴθειν, 'light up,'
'blaze')—a sense, indeed, appropriate to the appellative "Titan."
But this were quite a different sense than is usual in E., with
whom ether regularly stands for the element air. This, however, involves us in another difficulty: "moist air" (ὑγρὸς ἀήρ)
has been already mentioned; but with Zeller we may interpret
it as the lower, thicker, misty air (so ἀήρ in Homer), as op-
posed to the upper air, the pure ether, "without, however,
assuming any elemental difference," p. 786. "Moist air" is
rendered "feuchten Luftkreis" by Diels (FV), and "damp
mist" by Burnet. I may add that Burnet is evidently wrong
in affirming that ἀήρ never refers to air in E.: it is used inter-
changeably with αἰθήρ ('air') in fr. 100 (q. v.) Cf. Stickney,
notes to Cicero's De Nat. Deorum, I, 44.

"With Ether, the Titan who binds the globe about:"
cf.

"Bread, kingdoms, stars, and sky that holds them all."
Emerson, Days.

Fr. 39. The white Ether: "white" is not in the Greek, but is in
keeping with E.'s "Ether, the all splendorous," the "awful
heights of Air," the vaulted sky of his imagination.

As forsooth some tongues, etc.: a gruffness reminding of
Heraclitus, and of Emerson's line:

"The brave Empedocles defying fools."

Fr. 41. E. seems to have conceived the sun as "a luminous image of
the earth, when the latter was lighted up by the fire of the
day [i. e., the bright hemisphere] and reflected upon the crystal vault of heaven." Tannery, p. 317. But cf. Burnet, p. 254, and
Zeller, p. 789, for slight differences of interpretation. How
the sun, a mere reflection, was borne along its track in the revolving sky we are left to guess.

Fr. 42. An anticipation of the modern scientific explanation of solar eclipses.

The silver-eyed: γλαυκώπιδος μήνης; for the much discussed γλαυκῶπις see the Homeric dictionaries. It refers properly not to color but to "brightness and flashing splendor," used especially of Athene, of whom the Iliad (A, 200) says, "δεινὼ δέ οἱ ὄσσε φάανθεν." Cf. Schol. on Apoll. Rhod. 1. 1280 (quoted by Merrill and Riddell, Odys. A, 44): "διαγλαύσσουσιν ἀντὶ τοῦ φωτίζουσι ἢ διαλάμπουσι, ὅθεν καὶ ἡ Ἀθηνᾶ γλαυκῶπις, καὶ γλήνη ἡ κόρη τοῦ ὀφθαλμοῦ, παρὰ τὸ γλαύσσειν ὅ ἐστι λάμπειν. καὶ Εὐριπίδης ἐπὶ τῆς σελήνης ἐχρήσατο γλαυκῶπίς τε στρέφεται μήνη." But it is doubtful if E., who speaks of "Selene mild," intended here anything stronger than "with eye of silvery sheen."

γλαυκός is used of the willow, the olive, and E. himself uses it (fr. 93) of the elder. Diels' "blauäugigen" seems to me inadequate.

Fr. 43. E. knew the source of the moon's light (cf. fr. 45, 47); but the moon itself he held to be a disk of frozen air, and one-half as far from the earth as the sun ("E. διπλάσιον ἀπέχειν (τὸν ἥλιον) ἀπὸ τῆς γῆς ἥπερ τὴν σελήνην." Plac. II, 31).

Fr. 44. He darts his beams: with Diels I take the subject to be 'the sun' and not 'the earth' (Burnet); and "Olympos" is then the bright heaven, Tannery's "feu du jour" (see note to fr. 41). E. explained the light of the heavenly bodies through his doctrine of emanations, and, accordingly maintained—a correct conclusion from incorrect premises—that the sun's light requires a certain time to reach earth. Cf. Zeller, p. 790.

Fr. 46. Which round the outmost: probably 'goal is turning,' or something of the sort, followed here. The form of the clause shows that it served as a simile.

Fr. 47. Her lord: the sun, see note on fr. 43.

Fr. 48. E. conceived our earth as surrounded by a hollow globe composed of two hemispheres, a lighter of fire, a darker of air, whose revolution produces day and night. Cf. Zeller, p. 786 ff. This line means only that earth shuts off the light of the fiery hemisphere that sinks below the horizon, bearing with it its sun (see fr. 41).

Fr. 50. For authenticity cf. Diels, PPF. I am uncertain what scientific meaning this line had for Empedocles; but for the modern reader it is at least charming poetry. Burnet (p. 256) says: "Wind was explained from the opposite motions of the fiery and airy hemispheres. Rain was caused by the compression of the Air, which forced any water there might be in it out of its pores in the form of drops."

Fr. 51. *And upward,* etc.: of fire, which, in E.'s thought, had an upward, as air a downward (see fr. 54) tendency, innate powers apparently not elsewhere explained. The peculiar functions attributed by E. to fire led Aristotle (*De gen. et corr.,* B 3. 330b 19) to separate it from the other elements of the system, an interpretation developed with much ingenuity by Bodrero (Chap. II.).

Fr. 52. Doubtless an allusion to volcanic phenomena, as common in Sicily.

Fr. 53. "It" refers to air. "Met," i. e., with the other elements.

Fr. 54. See note to fr. 51.

Fr. 55. "The earth....was at first mixed with water, but the increasing compression caused by the velocity of the world's revolution [the Vortex of fr. 35] made the water gush forth." Burnet, p. 256. The phrase is not, then, as criticized by Aristotle, mere poetic metaphor.

Fr. 56. With E. fire has a crystallizing, condensing function. Cf. fr. 73.

Fr. 57-61. These fragments contain the rude germ of the theory of natural selection and the origin of species (but cf. Zeller, p. 795); they seem to refer to a process of animal genesis during the period when Love is increasing in power (i. e., the fourth period; see fr. 17); fr. 62, on the other hand to another process when Hate is increasing (i. e., in the period of the present world). Cf. Burnet, p. 261.

God with god: Gr. δαίμονι δαίμων, i. e., Love and Hate.

There seems to be no reason for the conjecture, sometimes advanced, that E. is here influenced by the monsters of Babylonian legend and art. The Greek imagination was long fa-

miliar with centaurs, satyrs, chimæras, cyclops, hermaphro-
dites and other "mixed shapes of being." The library of
Johns Hopkins has recently (1906) been enriched, so a medical colleague informs me, by a collection (originally from
Marburg), containing some 936 old volumes on monsters,
which the curious reader may consult at his leisure for further
parallels.

Fr. 62. See notes to fr. 57-61.

The sundered fire: Gr. κρινόμενον πῦρ, lit. 'self-sundering'
—the fire which "burns beneath the ground" and has the
"upward zeal." Though E. is speaking here of mankind,

"Of men and women, the pitied and bewailed,"

he probably considers the process as typical for the whole
animal kingdom.

Warm: warm and cold seem to have been important con-
ditions in E.'s system, the former favoring growth, the latter
inducing decay, old age, sleep, death, in the last instance perhaps serving as the occasion for the separation of the elements
by Hate. The general idea is probably as old as speculation.

Fr. 63. *For 'tis in part in man's*: i. e., in part in the male semen.
E. explained conception as a union of male and female semen,
each furnishing parts for the formation of offspring. Cf.

"Aegre admiscetur muliebri semine semen."
                              Lucr., IV, 1239.

In so far as this ancient belief recognizes that both sexes
furnish the germs of the offspring, it is an anticipation of
modern embryology.

Fr. 64. An alternative reading, a little freer:

"Love-longing comes upon him, waking well
Old memories, as he gazes."

Fr. 65. This is, perhaps, as rational as most modern theories. "At
present we are almost absolutely ignorant concerning the
causation of sex, though certain observers are inclined to
suppose that the determining factor must be sought for in the
ovum." Williams, *Obstetrics* (1904), p. 143.

Fr. 66. *Cloven meads*: surely the *labia majora*.

Fr. 68. *White pus*: Gr. τό πύον, not ὁ πῦός ('colostrum'), if my available lexical information be correct, though the latter is probably meant (Burnet). The comparison seems to be—however grotesque—between mother's milk (properly colostrum) in the breast enlarging during pregnancy, and the matter of a suppurating boil—the teat of the former corresponding to the "head" of the latter. Colostrum is, however, present in the breast after the first few months.

Fr. 69. *Twice-bearing*: i. e., bearing offspring in the seventh and tenth month.

Fr. 70. *Sheepskin*: used of the membrane conceived as covering the "embryo" (fœtus?). E. could only have been familiar with the membranes which follow the birth of the young.

Fr. 71. *Sun*: this is of course here a symbol for the element fire.

Fr. 73. *Kypris*: Aphrodite, Love.

> *To speed of fire that she might grow firm*: fire has a condensing property. Cf. fr. 56.

Fr. 74. The subject may be Aphrodite.

Fr. 75-76. Here the bones, the earthen part (in modern science, the lime) within some animals are related, quite in the spirit of our own physiology, to the shells on the outside of others. The turtle's shell, consisting chiefly of keratin, is, however, morphologically connected, like horn, finger-nails, etc., with the skin. Aristotle (*Pneumat.* 484a 38) says that E. explained fingernails as produced from sinew by hardening.

Fr. 77-78. Trees were supposed by E. to derive their nourishment through their pores from the air, more or less vitalizing according to the mixture—again a suggestion of modern science.

Fr. 79. In thus assimilating the seeds of the olive tree to the eggs laid by birds, E. was probably guided by similarity no less of function than of form.

Fr. 80. *Wherefore*: Can any one tell me? Prof. McGilvary happily suggests it is "because the pomegranate has a very hard thick skin, not admitting air as readily as the thin skin of an apple. See fr. 77-78."

Fr. 82. A doctrine of comparative morphology that has reminded many critics of the poet-scientist Goethe.

Fr. 84. *Of horny lantern*: the ancients had lanterns made of translucent horn, and "horny," though not in the text, must be understood here.

"Emp. conceives the eye as a sort of lantern. The apple of the eye contains fire and water enclosed in films, the pores of which, alternately arranged for each element, give to the emanations of each a free passage. Fire serves for perceiving the bright, water for the dark. When the emanations of visible things reach the outside of the eye, there pass through the pores from within it emanations of its fire and water, and from the joint meeting arises vision." Zeller, p. 801.

"It was an attempt, however inadequate, to explain perception by intermediate processes. It was an attempt, moreover, which admitted, however reluctantly, the subjective factor, thus completing one stage of the journey whose ultimate goal is to recognize that our sense-perceptions are anything rather than the mere reflections of exterior objective qualities of things." Gomperz, p. 235. Cf. Burnet, p. 267.

Fr. 86. *From which*: i. e., from these elements.

Fr. 87. *Bolts of love*: a metaphor for the uniting power of Aphrodite. Cf. fr. 96.

Fr. 88. Interesting as an early lesson in a sound theory of optics.

Fr. 89. Cf. note on fr. 2.

Fr. 90. *Sour sprung for Sour*: "went for" ($ἔβη$) would be a more effective rendering, but for the slangy connotations.

Fr. 92. Diels (FV), following Aristotle, who has preserved us the fragment, makes the connection sufficiently clear: "*Die Samenmischung bei der Erzeugung von Mauleseln bringt, da zwei weiche Stoffe zusammenkommen, eine harte Verbindung zustande. Denn nur Hohles and Dichtes passt zu einander. Dort aber geht es, wie wenn man Zinn und Kupfer mischt.*"

Fr. 93. *Silvery*: See note to fr. 42.

Fr. 94. Preserved only in Latin (Plut. *Quaest. nat.*, 39). Diels (PPF) has thus turned it into Greek:

"καὶ πέλει ἐν βένθει ποταμοῦ μέλαν ἐκ σκιόεντος
καὶ σπηλαιώδεσσιν ὁμῶς ἐνορᾶται ἐν ἄντροις."

Fr. 95. *They*: i. e., the eyes. The thought is thus completed by Diels (FV), following Simplicius: *"ergab sich auch der Unterschied, dass einige bei Tag, andere bei Nacht heller sehen."*

Fr. 96. Thus bones are formed of 2 parts earth, 2 parts water, and 4 parts fire.

Broad-breasted melting pots: "ben construtti vasi," as Bodrero translates it.

Glue of Harmony: cf. "bolts of love."

Fr. 97. Thus completed by Diels (FV), following Aristotle: *"hat ihre Form daher, dass sie bei der Entstehung der Tiere durch eine zufällige Wendung zerbrach."*

Fr. 98. *She met*: Gr. συνέκυρσε, a word, among others, which suggests in Empedocles' system, an implicit doctrine of chance. Cf. fr. 102, 103. Cf. Bodrero, p. 107 ff.

Ether, the all-splendorous: an illustration of how E. will sometimes emphasize a term, used symbolically to denote an element as one of the four-fold roots of all things, by an epithet suggestive of that element as it appears in the world about us.

Diels (PPF) paraphrases: "Tellus ad sanguinem efficiendum fere pares partes ignis, aquae, aeris arcessit, sed fieri potest ut paulo plus terrae aut minus, ut quae pluribus elementis una occurrat, admisceatur."

Fr. 99. *A fleshy sprout*: E.'s picturesque definition of the outer ear. The inner ear he likens to a bell which sounds as the air strikes upon it—again an anticipation of modern science.

Fr. 100. This fragment (cf. fr. 105) shows some knowledge of the motions of the blood, though far enough from the discovery of Harvey. Cf. Harvey's own work *On the Motion of the Heart and Blood in Animals* (1628) for the anterior views. As a theory of respiration, it is as grotesque as it is ingenious.

The comparison with the clepsydra, though in form of a Homeric simile, rests, as Burnet points out, upon scientific experiment, and is doubly significant for its sound physics. The following diagram and analysis from Burnet (p. 230) will, perhaps, make the allusion clear:

"The water escaped drop by drop through a single orifice at *a*. The top *b* was not altogether open, but was perforated so that the air might exert its pressure on the water inside. The instrument was filled by plunging it in water *upside down*, and stopping the orifice at *a* with the finger before taking it out again."

The water's destined bulk: i. e., a corresponding mass of water.

Fr. 101.   All that is left of E.'s theory of scent. The mites are the emanations.

Fr. 102.   *Got*: lit., "chanced on" (λελόγχασι). Cf. note on fr. 98.

Fr. 103.   *Chance*: cf. note on fr. 98. Here, as in some passages elsewhere, E. seems to be a hylozoist. Cf. Zeller, p. 802; but E. nowhere credits the elements as such, with consciousness, unless fr. 109 be so interpreted (but cf. Gomperz, p. 245).

Fr. 104.   *The lightest*: supply "bodies."

Fr. 105.   *In the blood streams*: cf. note to fr. 100.

The blood that stirs, etc.: the verse was often alluded to by the ancients (cf. Diels, PPF), and Tertullian seems himself to have turned it into Latin in his *De Anima* (chap. 16):

"namque homini sanguis circumcordialis et sensus."

But E. did not mean here, I think, to exclude some power of thought from other parts of the body; he says "where prevails the power," i. e., where it chiefly (μάλιστα) exists. Cf. Zeller, p. 803.

Fr. 106. Cf.

"Praeterea gigni pariter cum corpore et una
crescere sentimus pariterque senescere mentem."

Lucr., III, 445-6.

"Empedocles hat nicht die Seele aus den Elementen zusam-
mengesetzt, sondern er hat das, was wir Seelenthätigkeit nen-
nen, aus der elementarischen Zusammensetzung des Körpers
erklärt, eine vom Körper verschiedene Seele kennt seine Phy-
sik nicht"—i. e., a soul as distinct from the composition of the
elements in the body is nowhere found in the *On Nature*.
Zeller, p. 802.

Fr. 107. *These*: the elements. Cf. note on fr. 106.

Fr. 108. "By day" and "by night" have been supplied here from
references in Simpl. and Philop., quoted by Diels, PPF.

Fr. 109. *Through Earth,* etc.: "we think each element with the corresponding element in our body" (Zeller, p. 802), and the
same holds true of Love and Hate (cf. note on fr. 17).

Cf. Plotinus: Οὐ γὰρ ἂν πώποτε εἶδεν ὀφθαλμὸς ἥλιον ἡλιοειδὴς μὴ
γεγενημένος. Cf. also Goethe:

"Wär' nicht das Auge sonnenhaft,
Die Sonne könnt' es nie erblicken;
Läg' nicht in uns des Gottes eig'ne Kraft,
Wie könnt' uns Göttliches entzücken?"

Man is the microcosm.

Fr. 110. *All these things*: perhaps the good thoughts of the master's
doctrine; E. is here, as elsewhere, addressing Pausanias.

For of themselves....they grow, etc.: sound psychology, if
my interpretation just above be correct, and capable of serving
as the basis for a chapter in the philosophy of living, on the
practical bearings upon character of right and wrong thinking.

All things have fixed intent: i. e., consciousness.

Fr. 111. *Drugs*: Gr. φάρμακα; possibly "charms" is better, as suggested to me by a friend. Galen makes E. the founder of the
Italian school of medicine. Cf. Burnet, p. 215.

The dominion over human ills, sickness, windstorms, drought
and death, here promised to Pausanias, was early imputed to

Empedocles himself (cf. *Introduction*), perhaps, chiefly by virtue of these lines.

The might of perished men: Gr. καταφθιμένου μένος ἀνδρός. "Spirits of the dead" seems hardly permissible with μένος (though the word is sometimes used of the spirit, the courage of man), and would render still more crass the contradiction with what E. has elsewhere told us in the *On Nature* of the psychic life. One would conjecture that the fragment belongs to the *Purifications*, but for the fact that it is addressed to Pausanias, and not, as the latter, to the citizens of Acragas.

THE PURIFICATIONS.

The inconsistency of the religious tenets of this poem with the philosophic system of the *On Nature* is, like the relation between the two parts of Parmenides' poem, a commonplace in the history of Greek thought; and, though attempts at a reconciliation have been made, conservatively by Burnet (p. 271), radically by Bodrero (passim), our materials seem too scanty for anything more than ingenious speculation. The work evidently owes much to Orphic and Pythagorean tradition; but there seems no reason for doubting its genuineness.

Fr. 112. *The yellow Acragas*: The river beside the walls of Agrigentum.

As god immortal now: an Orphic line runs:

"Happy and blessèd, shalt thou be a god and no longer a mortal."

Cf. Harrison, *Proleg. to Study of Greek Religion*, p. 589.

Crowned both with fillets and with flowering wreaths: Empedocles' passage about the Sicilian cities reminds one of the peasant-prophet who went about the populous towns of Galilee, followed by the multitudes seeking a sign or a healing word; but the simplicity of the Jew is more impressive than the display of the Greek.

Fr. 113. I. e., "Why should I boast of my miracles and my following, who am a god and so much above mankind?" E., if an Orphic (cf. Burnet, p. 213, and his references), has here little of even "the somewhat elaborate and self-conscious humility" of his sect.

Fr. 115. *With amplest oaths*: cf. fr. 30.

Those far spirits: Gr. δαίμονες; Burnet (p. 269) identifies these with "the long-lived gods" of the *On Nature*.

With slaughter: i. e., bloodshed of animals, no less than of fellowmen; it probably refers also to the eating of flesh. Cf. fr. 136.

In offense: in sin, sinfully.

Thrice ten thousand....years: Gr. τρὶς μύριαι ὧραι, by some interpreted as 10,000 years. Cf. Zeller, p. 780.

Be born through time, etc.: the doctrine of metempsychosis in E. is probably Pythagorean in origin, though apparently not entirely Pythagorean in form: "Non è specializzata solo a certi determinati esseri, ma riguarda tutti gli esseri organici e giunge sino agli Dei," according to Bodrero (p. 146).

For now Air hunts them, etc.: Here we have mention of the familiar four elements, and below of Hate, but the realm of the Blessed and the curse pronounced upon the spirits seem incompatible with the *On Nature*. Moreover, something is needed after all for metemphychosis besides "the reappearance of the same corporeal elements in definite combinations" (Burnet, p. 271), though perhaps Empedocles deemed that sufficient. Cf. the Buddhistic doctrine of reincarnation and retribution. Cf. also Gomperz, p. 249 ff.

Fr. 116. *Charis*: Aphrodite. In the *On Nature* (fr. 35) E. refers to the unwillingness also of Hate to submit to the law of necessity.

Fr. 117. Possibly as a punishment for having tasted flesh: "Empedocle ci fa sapere che il suo spirito era già pervenuto alla sede dei beati, ma che cedendo alla tentazione accostò impuri cibi agli labbri [cf. fr. 139], e tornò ad essere arbusto, pesce, uccello, fanciullo e giovinetta." Bodrero, p. 147.

"So long as man [in the Orphic belief] has not severed completely his brotherhood with plants and animals, not realized the distinctive marks and attributes of his humanity, he will say with Empedocles:

'Once on a time a youth was I, and I was a maiden,
A bush, a bird, and a fish with scales that gleam in the
ocean.' "

Harrison, *Proleg. to Study of Greek Religion,* p. 590.

Fr. 118. This must refer to Empedocles' feelings, as he entered,
after banishment from heaven, upon his earthly career (cf. fr.
119). Cf.

"Infans. . . .
vagituque locum lugubri complet, ut æqumst
cui tantum in vita restet transire malorum."

Lucr., V, 226.

For other parallels see Munro and Guissani, notes to loc. cit.

Fr. 119. Cf. note to fr. 118.

Fr. 121. *A joyless land*: with fr. 122 and 123 this refers, as I understand it, to our mundane world itself.

And Labors burthened with the water-jars: this is a paraphrase of the puzzling ἔργα ῥευστά, which, it has been suggested to me by Prof. Newbold, "can hardly be anything other
than the fruitless toil of the water-carriers, representing, if
the scene be earth, life's disappointments and the vanity of all
human pursuits." If this interpretation be correct, the figure
is evidently taken from the conception of the Orphic Hell,
which, if the literary tradition be reliable, was situated upon
earth (for water-carriers in Hell, cf. Harrison, *Proleg. to
Study of Greek Religion,* Chap. XI, p. 614 ff.) ; but that E. is
depicting scenes from the Orphic Hell itself may be ques-
tioned from what is preserved to us of the context : he seems
throughout these adjacent fragments to be dwelling on the
earthly abiding place unto which he and others must descend
from the realm of the blessed.

But Diels (PPF) : "nec sunt humanae *res fluxae* (Karsten)
nec vero *foedum morbi genus* (Stein), sed *agri inundationibus
vexati.*" According to this, it might run in English :

"And slimy floods of wasting waters rise
And wander," etc.

Cf.

"Lightning and Inundation vexed the plains."
Shelley, *Prometheus Unbound,* I, 169.

Fr. 122.   *There*: i. e., in the joyless land," the "roofèd cave," this earth.

Virgin of the Sun: the moon(?).

The personages that follow are feminine.   E. evidently imitates the catalogue of Nymphs in Il. Σ 39:

" ἔνθ' ἄρ' ἔην Γλαύκη τε, Θάλειά τε Κυμοδόκη τε".... κτλ,

Fr. 125.   This refers, perhaps, to the passage from the life, of the blessed to the (relative) death on this earth, where souls are wrapped

"in unfamiliar tunics of the flesh" (fr. 126.),
and have a hapless existence.

Fr. 126.   This refers to metempsychosis.

Fr. 127.   *The worthiest dwellings*: for those who have proceeded in their purification; expanded from the context where the original passage is found (in Ael. *nat. an.*, XII, 7., quoted by Diels, PPF) : "λέγει δὲ καὶ Ἐ. τὴν ἀρίστην εἶναι μετοίκησιν τὴν τοῦ ἀνθρώπου, εἰ μὲν ἐς ζῷον ἡ λῆξις αὐτὸν μεταγάγοι, λέοντα γίνεσθαι· εἰ δὲ ἐς φυτόν, δάφνην." E. conceived the plants as having souls, a fancy not confined to antiquity.

Fr. 128.   A Golden Age seems incompatible with the biology of the *On Nature*, but cf. Burnet (p. 271), who thinks it to be referred to the time when Hate was just beginning to separate the elements.

Kydoimos: personification of uproar, as in battle.

Unmixed blood: the figure is from unmixed wine, which, as such, is thick and dark.

Fr. 129.   "Similiter mentis infinitam vim (philosophi scilicet non vatis) Parmenides praedicat fr. 2 λεῦσσε δ' ὅμως ἀπεόντα νόωι παρεόντα βεβαίως κτλ. unde apparet cur nonnulli Parmenidem hic respici arbitrati sunt.   nec dubium cur Pythagorae quater redivivi mentio ["a reference to Pythagoras, four times returned to life"] facta sit."   Diels, PPF.   But Burnet (p. 236), conjecturing that E. is still speaking of the Golden Age, thinks the "supreme man" is Orpheus.

In ten or twenty human ages: cf. paraphrase of Diels (PPF) : "ubi summa vi mentem intenderat, facile singula quae-

cumque sive decem sive viginti hominum saeculis fiebant per-
spicere solebat."

Fr. 132. Bodrero in his attempt to interpret harmoniously all the
thoughts of Empedocles explains this passage with reference
to what has gone before in the *On Nature* as follows: "Felice
colui che ha una così perfetta composizione di elementi da
poter comprendere la natura degli Dei; misero chi per la
povertà delle proprie risorse, segue le credenze superstiziose
e comuni" (p. 159).

Fr. 134. Cf. fr. 29 and note. Burnet thinks that E. is here too
speaking of the Sphere; but the last lines seem out of place
in such a connection, even though we recall that E. has vaguely
named the Sphere "God" (fr. 31).

Fr. 135. *Broad-ruling Ether*, etc.: "den weithin herrschenden Feuer-
aether und den unermesslichen Himmelsglanz." Diels, FV.
Cf. note to fr. 38.

   Din of slaughter: killing of animals. Cf. fr. 137 and 115.
The reader need hardly be reminded of the Orphic interdict
against eating animal food.

Fr. 138. "As our philosopher placed life and soul in the blood [cf.
fr. 105], it was not unnatural for him to speak of 'drawing the
soul.'" Diels, PPF. The passage seems to refer either to
the draining or scooping up into a bronze vessel of the blood
of slaughtered animals, or to cutting their throats with a
sacrificial knife of bronze.

Fr. 139. Cf. note on fr. 117.

Fr. 140. For the probable reason of this injunction cf. fr. 127.

Fr. 141. A familiar Pythagorean commandment, on the meaning of
which scholars have offered a variety of suggestions. Bodrero
(p .149) and others connect it with the doctrine of metempsychosis (cf. fr. 139, 127); Burnet (p. 104) well compares it
(and kindred Pythagorean rules) to the bizarre taboos of
savages. Possibly there was some fancied association, based
on shape, with the egg (as E. likened olives to eggs in fr. 79),
which, as may be gathered from Plutarch, was held by Orphics
and Pythagoreans to be taboo, perhaps as being the principle

of life (cf. Harrison, *Proleg. to Study of Greek Religion*, p. 628).

Fr. 142. "etiam sensus incertus, utrum Iovis et Hecates regna (cf. fr. 135, 2?) opponantur an quattuor elementa, unde exclusus sit scelestus (cf. fr. 115, 9)." Diels, PPF.

Fr. 143. *Scooping*: Gr. ταμόντ', 'cutting,' i. e., water for purposes of ceremonial lustration(?), for which bronze vessels were regularly employed.

Fr. 144. George Herbert uses the same figure somewhere in his poems.

Fr. 145. *Evil doings*: presumably such "sin" as referred to above which doom souls to

"be born through time
In various shapes of mortal kind which change
Ever and ever paths of troublous life." Fr. 115.

Fr. 146-7. The last words left us of the all too few on the transmigration of the soul.

Fr. 148. This does not refer to "mother earth," but to the human body, "τὸ τῆι ψυχῆι περικείμενον σῶμα" (Plut. *Quaest. Conviv.* V 8, 2, p. 683 E [*post* fr. 80], quoted by Diels, PPF).

Fr. 149. Of air.

Fr. 151. Of Aphrodite.

Fr. 152. Preserved in Aristotle's Poetics, 21, quoted by Diels, PPF.

Fr. 153. Gr. βαυβώ, a very rare word: "σημαίνει δὲ καὶ κοιλίαν ὡς παρ' Ἐμπεδοκλεῖ." Hesych., quoted by Diels, PPF.

Fr. 153a. Diels (FV) translates the doxographer: "*In* sieben mal sieben Tagen *wird der Embryo (seiner Gliederung nach) durchgebildet.*"